D1431001

PR/

ADAPTIVE SELLING

"There's no question about the value of SOCIAL STYLE. I can tell you unequivocally and without a doubt that if it hadn't been for the Style training I took, I wouldn't be where I am today and have had the career success I have enjoyed. There's just no way. It has been that one critically important skill that I think has made all the difference for me."

Jim Knauss II, Global Markets Leader, People Advisory Services, EY

"Many of the sales processes and methods in the market today are fine and they can work. What they typically do not address is EQ, the softer set of selling skills that are required to be consistently successful in sales. And that comes at you from different dimensions. It's not just the client interactions. It's the pursuit team that you build on the selling side. It's the delivery leadership team and how they mirror the client from a SOCIAL STYLE standpoint, demographically, and from an organization-accountability perspective."

John Maguire, Senior Vice President Sales, Chief Sales Officer, Cognizant

"If you could gain the magical interpersonal skills that would instantly enhance your ability to connect with your customers and co-workers like never before, would you be interested? If I said the same skills would also drive enhanced relationships with your friends and family, what would you say? TRACOM's SOCIAL STYLE and Versatility provide the Social Intelligence a person needs to honestly and authentically improve rapport, demonstrate enhanced leadership, and connect with those they interact with on a regular basis."

Mike Miller, Sr. Manager Learning & Development, Reynolds American, Inc.

"SOCIAL STYLE is unquestionably a very powerful way of looking at the world. It's clear, it's memorable, and it's something that you can apply quickly as opposed to many other models. You only need to remember four Styles and how to work with each of them. Even in the heat of the moment you can quickly apply SOCIAL STYLEs to build a productive relationship."

Peter Matthews, Senior Partner

adaptive
SELLING
how to succeed during times of disruption

adaptive
SELLING
how to succeed during times of disruption

DAVID COLLINS & JOHN R. MYERS

www.BookpressPublishing.com

Published in Des Moines, Iowa, by:

BookPress Publishing
P.O. Box 71532, Des Moines, IA 50325
www.BookPressPublishing.com

Publisher's Cataloging-in-Publication Data

Names: Collins, David, 1967-, author. | Myers, John R., author.
Title: Adaptive selling : how to succeed during times of disruption /
David Collins and John R. Myers.
Description: Includes bibliographical references. | Des Moines, IA: BookPress Publishing, 2021.
Identifiers: LCCN: 2020916369 | ISBN: 978-1-947305-19-9
Subjects: LCSH Selling. | Success in business. | Communication. | Interpersonal communication. | Interpersonal relations. | Business communication. | BISAC BUSINESS & ECONOMICS / Sales & Selling / General
Classification: LCC HF5438.25 .C645 2021 | DDC 658.85--dc23

First Edition

Printed in the United States of America
10 9 8 7 6 5 4 3 2 1

This book would not have been possible without the groundbreaking work of our founders, the ongoing support of our clients who have incorporated TRACOM's solutions into their sales organizations all across the globe, the people of TRACOM both past and present, and the entire community of several thousand SOCIAL STYLE certified facilitators who train hundreds of thousands of people each year.

We wish to acknowledge the contributions made decades ago to the field of behavioral science by TRACOM's Founders, Dr. David Merrill and Roger Reid. It was their original research and development that led to the creation of the SOCIAL STYLE Model. We hope that David and Roger would be very proud of the company they started as it has continued to advance their research to increase its impact across the globe. TRACOM has become the leading provider of critical soft skills solutions that have been proved to make a difference in performance and success. We are proud that millions of people around the world have used TRACOM to uncover hidden barriers to their performance and identify strategies that enable more positive outcomes and professional success.

We would like to especially thank all our clients in over 100 countries where our solutions are used. We especially thank Jim Knauss, Peter Matthews, Nancy Kopp, David Bruesehoff, Tracy Embro, Andrew Wright, John Maguire, Ernie Smith, Henry "Hawk" Macintosh, Mike Miller, Fred Dulin, Anita Natesh, and Tony Sammut for sharing their stories and insights into how TRACOM has benefitted them and their organizations.

CONTENTS

introduction

One of the most common questions we are asked by senior executives is, "What makes a top sales performer?" What makes certain people in a wide range of industries so successful at consistently winning big deals while others fail or only achieve sub-par outcomes? Is their success due to random chance, genetics, or do they simply do things differently from less successful sales people?

This is usually quickly followed by, "What do you think is the best sales methodology to deploy? Is it Strategic Selling, Challenger Selling, Relationship Selling, or another one of the sales processes on the market?" This is not an easy question to answer because there are sales people who succeed and who fail using each of the models. So it must be more than just choosing a sales process.

Equally important to these questions in today's world is, "Will the characteristics and processes of the most popular selling approaches still be relevant in the world of selling and buying, given all the systemic disruptions that are occurring?"

How many of these have you experienced?

- Customers using technology and social media to gather

information—get peer reviews, find competitive offerings, and locate pricing data without any interaction with a sales person.

• A pervasive customer attitude of "Don't contact us...we will call you...maybe."

• Buying decisions being made or directed by globalized buying or project teams rather than being limited to individual stakeholders or procurement professionals.

• Increasingly complex sales cycles that require a team-selling approach with more and more clients.

• Internal demand for use of CRM systems, marketing automation, and other analytical tools that reduce sales people's time building real connections with clients.

Starting in the early 2000s, we began to work with several high-level sales and business development professionals across a variety of global companies. They used a wide range of differing sales methodologies. They were all unique individuals and worked in many different industries in different cultures all over the world. Yet they all shared a common set of characteristics. And they were all highly successful! As we got to know them better, we realized that many of these individuals had also failed in sales at one point in their career. What changed? How did they learn the secret of how to sell so successfully? What were they doing differently from earlier in their careers when they struggled, and why was it working? Would these learnings help us all to adapt to the seismic changes occurring in the sales world?

Over the last several years at TRACOM, we have researched these issues to understand what these top performers had in common and to determine if these skill sets could be learned and applied by others. This book is a summary of what we have learned. It is designed to help you, the sales professional, to learn about and apply the key behaviors of top sales performers.

This book would not have been possible without the ongoing support of our clients who have incorporated TRACOM's solutions into their sales organizations. We would like to thank Jim Knauss, Peter Matthews, Nancy Kopp, David Bruesehoff, Tracy Embo, Andrew Wright, John Maguire, Ernie Smith, Henry "Hawk" Macintosh, Mike Miller, Fred Dulin, Anita Natesh, and Tony Sammut for sharing their stories and insights into how TRACOM has benefitted them and their organizations. Without our hundreds of client firms across the globe, this book would not have been possible.

David Collins
CEO TRACOM Group

John R. Myers
Chairman TRACOM Group

How is this Book Different?

This book will show how the Adaptive Selling approach uniquely integrates the following:

• The importance of properly managing relationships during the selling process.

• The most commonly used sales processes including Spin Selling, Consultative Selling, Challenger Selling, and many others.

• TRACOM's proprietary and empirically researched SOCIAL STYLE Model as a tool for enhancing any Sales Methodology.

• Advanced sales tools and strategies like Decision Mapping, Win-Loss Reviews, and Meeting Preparation.

You will find many formidable books on several of these topics—for example, The Versatility Factor and Personal Styles and Effective Performance as well as various Sales Application Guides from TRACOM, books on Solution Selling and SPIN from Huthwaite, Miller Heiman's work around account strategies, and newer works such as Challenger Sales from The Corporate Executive Board along with Insight Selling from RAIN Group. There are also Decision Mapping/Power Mapping approaches and tools from such providers as Salesforce.com, Altify, and Demand Metric. What you can't find is a book that integrates these various methods and skills together as simply and applicably as this one does.

In addition, this book takes SOCIAL STYLE to places that you likely won't find elsewhere, such as Messaging and Organizing Meetings and even doing Win-Loss Reviews by Style. SOCIAL

STYLE is embedded into all sections as it is the key to Adaptive Selling and such areas as Baggage Handling, Decision Mapping, Preparing for Important Meetings and Presentations, and conducting Win-Loss Reviews.

TRACOM didn't invent all of these techniques. What we have done is provide an application that increases the power and usefulness of any set of selling skills across all of the most popular sales process methodologies of today. In TRACOM's fifty-plus years pursuing competitive deals, we have learned first-hand which techniques work and can be integrated together with positive results. And so have our many global clients who have successfully implemented Adaptive Selling within their companies. This book is based on what has proved to work in a variety of marketplaces.

Who Benefits from This Book?

Most obviously, individuals and organizations with the challenges listed earlier will benefit from the methods detailed in this book. The skills and applications described in this book can improve the chances of winning large, complex deals. In consulting terms, this complexity refers to the competitive nature of deals as well as the presence of multiple members on both the selling and buying teams. The techniques and skills apply just as well to smaller, less complex sales with only one buyer.

Sales professionals and account teams will also find this book useful in terms of better understanding their clients and how to build better and deeper relationships with them. It will also provide insight into how to evaluate the client situation and how to select the appropriate sales approach.

Types of organizations that can benefit most from this book

because of the nature of their marketplaces include:

- Professional Services
- Consulting
- Systems Integration Services
- Software Providers
- Technology Providers
- Finance and Banking
- Insurance
- Investment Banking
- Consumer Goods
- Hospitality
- Pharmaceuticals
- Retail
- Medical Equipment
- Commercial Real Estate
- Manufacturing
- Legal

THE CHANGING DYNAMICS
OF BUYING AND SELLING

The Case for Becoming an Adaptive Sales Person

Over the past twenty-five years, the Internet has reshaped the worlds of retailing, publishing, entertainment, and information along with many others in ways that your parents may never have imagined. These changes are now appearing in the world of selling and buying and causing seismic disruptions at an increasingly rapid pace. This "brave new world" requires new skills to survive and prosper. Sales professionals must adapt! And to become more adaptive we need to start by understanding some of the changes that are occurring and which skill sets will be needed.

The State of Sales 2018 report from LinkedIn provides insight into why we must learn to sell adaptively versus being constrained by a specific sales methodology.

> *"B2B sales has never been more challenging. Highly per-sonalized services like Netflix and Amazon are driving customers to expect more from the brands they interact with, including those with B2B sales teams. Millennials,*

who have especially high expectations for personalization, are gaining influence in the workforce and will make up 46 percent of professionals by 2020."

Sellers today must meet these heightened expectations while building consensus among a larger group of stake-holders: the average buyer's circle is now 6.8 people. They must also team up with their marketing counterparts to reach each of these individuals at every stage of the path to purchase. To be successful in modern sales, you need to build relationships at scale tapping into advanced sales technology to engage with the right contacts faster, while fostering human connection and trust."[1]

State of Sales 2018, published by LinkedIn, August 2018

If you are in sales or procurement, you are experiencing changes that are creating tectonic shifts in the landscapes of selling and buying. For the unprepared, these changes threaten careers, economic futures, and long-held beliefs about the very nature of selling and buying. So is this the demise of selling and buying as they have played out for the past 150 years?

Let's consider some of the types of tremors and shocks that have been occurring in the world of sales people and their buyers over the past twenty years and consider how they have impacted you and your organization:

• Technology has given birth to digitization, CRM, blogs, webinars, video conferencing, Facebook, Twitter, LinkedIn, and social media which have sent seismic changes throughout the selling and buying processes.

• Today's procurement professionals are independent,

demanding, and connected with others in their industries and make decisions based on lots of information including third-party reviews, endorsements, and critiques.

• Customers are regularly seeking and finding information and alternative suppliers themselves without engaging with any sales person at early stages of a purchasing process.

• A move toward project-based and team-based procurement efforts comprised of employees across multiple geographies and disciplines and the corresponding demand for team-based sales approaches.

• Major sales now require multiple meetings where sales people need to do more listening than talking, more discovery, more team-based selling, and dealing with more multi-buyer situations and the need to create more individualized solutions.

• Follow-up is no longer a thank-you note or holiday gift, but a series of technology-supported communications that are quicker and more efficient to execute and capable of continuing personalized, ongoing contact with the customer(s).

And what about the very personal level of disruption that has been occurring between the sales person and their buyer? If you're a sales person relying solely on your interpersonal skills, your knowledge of the company's products, and your negotiation ability to gain access to customers, you may be in trouble. Here is how you will know.

Are you experiencing any of the following symptoms?

• The client has a standardized buying process, and they have little time or inclination to meet with you.

• You're no longer dealing with individual decision-makers with unique needs and the latitude to call their own shots.

• Your clients are not asking about the features and benefits of your products and services. That's what the Internet is for, they say!

• They are expecting you to bring new and unique ideas specific to their business.

• It seems that every decision isn't based on the value of your solution or your knowledge of the customer, but is based more on competitive comparison and price.

Amidst all these disruptions, sales people need to see that the future does not have to be so scary.

As a sales professional, you have a bright future ahead of you if you can respond to key trends in the B2B world. Each trend offers an opportunity to develop a new skill for sales professionals and adopt a new practice. Because these practices are not yet "best practices," Gouillart and Quancard refer to them as "next practices,"[2] in that they are likely to become best practices over time. They are already at work in the most innovative companies. Each of them offers an opportunity to add new value.

Let's consider some of these trends and corresponding next practices and how they may impact you.

Trend #1: The Problems that Companies' Sales and Procurement People are Asked to Tackle are Broader and More Complex than Ever

- **Next Practice #1:** *Sales and Procurement Professionals Work Together to Address New Problems of Increasing Magnitude*

  What this means for you is that you will need to think more strategically about client challenges and present innovative solutions to address them rather than an "out of the box" standard offering. In order to be innovative, you will need to build more trust with your customers to learn more information about the problems and challenges they are facing. And as you will learn in a later chapter, you will need to overcome cognitive biases in order to win.

Trend #2: Sales and Procurement Networks are Becoming More Diffuse and Complex

- **Next Practice #2:** *Sales and Procurement Professionals Organize Problem-Solving Networks Across Company Boundaries*

  You will need to master the skills of networking across client organizations as well as within your own in order to be able to navigate complex opportunities. And you need to learn how to influence others toward a common goal.

Trend #3: People Expect Problems to Be Solved in Real Time as a Group

- **Next Practice #3:** *Sales and Procurement Professionals Must Structure a Process and Platform for Live Cross-Company Engagement*

You will need to build trusting relationships with more people both in person and via technology that earn you the right to be considered a strategic asset for developing and implementing creative solutions. And you will need to enhance your ability to operate with increased resiliency and agility to accomplish this goal.

Trend #4: Big Data Has Arrived in Sales and Procurement

- **Next Practice #4:** *Sales and Procurement Professionals Facilitate the Development of New Data-Driven, Cross-Company Interactions Fed by Digital Platforms*

  You will need to do deep dives into increasingly complex sets of data using a multitude of tools and facilitating and participating in cross-functional and cross-company project teams. You will need to know how to quickly understand the way people prefer to interact with others, use their time, and make decisions.

Trend #5: Sales and Procurement Professionals Use Their Own Transformation to Transform the Work Experience of Others

- **Next Practice #5:** *Sales and Procurement Professionals Facilitate the Creation of New Personal Experiences for Individuals in Their Network*

  You will need to gain insight into the strengths and preferences of clients and colleagues and actively seek to engage them in projects through building and facilitating mutually beneficial relationships.

Trend #6: Sales and Procurement Professionals Are Asked to Constantly Reinvent the Business Model of Their Firms

- **Next Practice #6:** *Sales and Procurement Professionals Find New Sources of Value for Their Firms*

  You will need to shift your focus from sharing product knowledge to a much more complex understanding of your client, their industry and marketplace, their competitors, and use that knowledge to anticipate, create, and deliver new and meaningful solutions that the client themselves may not have seen as possible. You will also need to learn how the various individuals engaged in the decision deal with risk, data requirements, and other key decision factors and how to communicate about all of these things appropriately with each individual.

These six trends point to a stark choice for senior account managers and procurement folks alike. Either they adapt to the new reality of selling and buying, or they will be replaced by web-based or channel-based alternatives that will do most of what they do today at a fraction of the cost. Increasingly, there is no middle ground. Sales and procurement either evolve into high-value-added sales and procurement professionals or disappear. And to make this reality happen, a core set of Adaptive Selling skills will need to be mastered.

What Sales Methodology is Best in the Emerging Reality of Selling and Buying?

Over the past 60 years, selling has moved through distinct approaches. Initially, sales started off by focusing on the product and the price, before moving on to feature benefit selling, and then on to need-satisfaction selling. It later expanded into solution selling and then consultative/strategic/value-selling and most recently to insightful/challenger selling. Each of these approaches demanded that sales professionals develop new skills, sharpen old skills, think differently, undergo new training, and use new technologies and methods. Each of these new approaches resulted from changes in what customers buy, why they buy it, where they buy it, and how they buy it.

> *"I think that sales methods or process-program methodologies are all pretty much the same. Just some few minor differences, since they're really about how do you understand your client or customer before you go meet with them. How do you make sure you ask really good questions? How do you provide insight? How do you develop mutually agreed next steps that then turn into opportunities for you? They used slightly different words or points of focus but are, in reality, very much the same thing. What is important, regardless of what sales process or approach you use, is knowing how to adapt it to the person you are attempting to influence towards some kind of decision whether it is a purchase or just agreeing to another meeting."*
>
> **— Jim Knauss II**
> **Global Markets Leader, People Advisory Services – EY**

As the third decade of the twenty-first century arrives, key modifications are emerging to these various methods in response to changes in their customers, organizations, people, and their market environments. Already top performers are getting a jump-start on the skills, processes, and technologies that will allow them to continue to be high-performing sales professionals in this new marketplace. The remainder of this book shares the key characteristics of top performing sales professionals regardless of the sales situation they encounter. And it will present new skills as well as how to maximize the skills and methodologies readers have already developed!

So what is the focus of this type of sales? Simply put, it revolves around the ability of sales professionals to demonstrate Adaptive Selling. Going forward, sales professionals need their skills to be flexible enough to apply the most appropriate sales methodology based on the type of situational and behavioral demands their clients present.

The world of Adaptive Selling will demand discipline, speed, creativity, risk-taking, resiliency, trust, and the ability to work with and influence a wide range of people who have different preferences across a range of situations. According to LinkedIn, 40 percent of sales professionals rank trust as the number one factor in closing deals and 51 percent of decision makers rank trust as the top factor they desire in a salesperson. Adaptive Selling is the key to achieving trust.

> *"And the only way that I can drive the type of initiatives that I do in my job is to build a large, powerful network and have really strong relationships. That takes the ability to be versatile and adaptable, because nothing works without a trusting relationship!"*
>
> **— Nancy Kopp:** EY Americas

The following chart gives an understanding of the methodologies that developed over the last 60 years and the order in which they were developed. It walks through the key focus of each of the methodologies, where and when each methodology is best used, and also cites the training firms associated with the development of the methodology. Spend some time reviewing the chart to see where you may have some skill gaps, because going forward top sales professionals will need to be skilled at applying all of these methodologies.

The Main Principles of Adaptive Selling

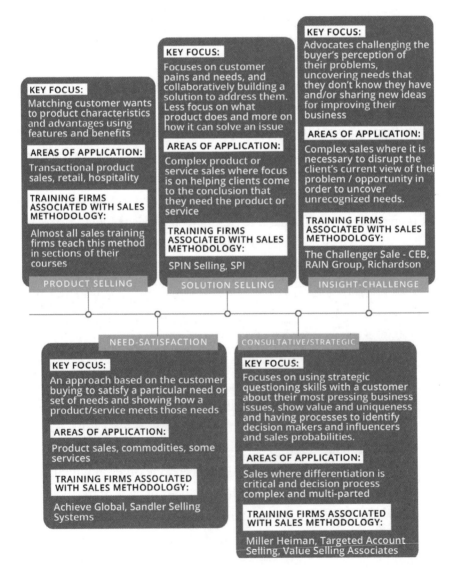

KEY FOCUS:
Matching customer wants to product characteristics and advantages using features and benefits

AREAS OF APPLICATION:
Transactional product sales, retail, hospitality

TRAINING FIRMS ASSOCIATED WITH SALES METHODOLOGY:
Almost all sales training firms teach this method in sections of their courses

PRODUCT SELLING

KEY FOCUS:
Focuses on customer pains and needs, and collaboratively building a solution to address them. Less focus on what product does and more on how it can solve an issue

AREAS OF APPLICATION:
Complex product or service sales where focus is on helping clients come to the conclusion that they need the product or service

TRAINING FIRMS ASSOCIATED WITH SALES METHODOLOGY:
SPIN Selling, SPI

SOLUTION SELLING

KEY FOCUS:
Advocates challenging the buyer's perception of their problems, uncovering needs that they don't know they have and/or sharing new ideas for improving their business

AREAS OF APPLICATION:
Complex sales where it is necessary to disrupt the client's current view of their problem / opportunity in order to uncover unrecognized needs.

TRAINING FIRMS ASSOCIATED WITH SALES METHODOLOGY:
The Challenger Sale - CEB, RAIN Group, Richardson

INSIGHT-CHALLENGE

NEED-SATISFACTION

CONSULTATIVE/STRATEGIC

KEY FOCUS:
An approach based on the customer buying to satisfy a particular need or set of needs and showing how a product/service meets those needs

AREAS OF APPLICATION:
Product sales, commodities, some services

TRAINING FIRMS ASSOCIATED WITH SALES METHODOLOGY:
Achieve Global, Sandler Selling Systems

KEY FOCUS:
Focuses on using strategic questioning skills with a customer about their most pressing business issues, show value and uniqueness and having processes to identify decision makers and influencers and sales probabilities.

AREAS OF APPLICATION:
Sales where differentiation is critical and decision process complex and multi-parted

TRAINING FIRMS ASSOCIATED WITH SALES METHODOLOGY:
Miller Heiman, Targeted Account Selling, Value Selling Associates

In the age of smart machines and artificial intelligence, the old definition of what makes a person smart and effective doesn't make sense anymore. There is no way any human being can out-calculate a computer. The new intelligence in selling will be determined not by what you know, but rather by the quality of your listening, relating, collaborating, changing, communicating, and creating skills. It will require you to understand your unconscious biases and how to manage them. Think of these skills as promoting higher levels of human relationships and emotional engagement, which is what we call Social Intelligence. It is also the key to Adaptive Selling. It is no longer just about one's basic cognitive intelligence and having great products. It is now all about using Social Intelligence as you go about gaining your client's commitment. The next chapters will define these critical constructs and help you apply them to your career.

So will it make a difference? The research for this book involved interviewing a number of senior sales professionals and executives from large global companies. Throughout this book, we will share their comments on how Adaptive Selling has impacted their organizations as well as themselves.

One individual we worked with had over 40 years in sales and sales training in both technology and professional service firms. While recognized as a "Rainmaker" by his company for his individual performance, eventually he added a role as a "Sales Coach" for large pursuits. Generally, this meant working on "Mega Deals": those classified as $50 million or larger. The approach he took to coaching sales teams pursuing these deals was to apply the methodologies presented in Adaptive Selling. And it paid off for everyone. When asked for a highlight from his sales team coaching experience using the Adaptive Selling approach, he shared that, "We had a significantly higher competitive win rate when pursuit teams I coached using these approaches applied them to the opportunity, with the two biggest wins being over 1.5 billion dollars each." While your situation may revolve around smaller pursuits, if you apply what you will learn in Adaptive Selling, you will increase your win rate!

Selecting the Methodology

To achieve real success in Adaptive Selling, professionals need skills for diagnosing the situational and behavioral demands their clients present. They then need to apply the most appropriate methodology based on their client's preferences and their situation. Without this flexibility to use the most appropriate sales processes, clients will turn to competitors who are more flexible in responding to their goals. At the simplest level, sales people in situations such as commodity, retail, and mass market selling will need skills at persuading and presenting features and benefits of their products. At the most sophisticated level, sales people will need to focus on investigating their clients' business threats and opportunities. They will need to design innovative ways for clients to apply the sales professional's offerings to meet these challenges while using proven practices to energize clients as well as the sales professional's team around these innovative applications. The days of having to be proficient with a single sales methodology are over. Sales professionals need to be able to use all of them depending on the situation.

Social Intelligence and Cognitive Biases

Social Intelligence skills accentuate our human capabilities and set us apart from artificial intelligence. But, similar to technical skills, they do not come naturally to most of us. In fact, we are hindered by a wide range of cognitive biases that distort how we Think, Act, and React to the world around us, and this affects our performance. All people are affected by cognitive biases. Why? Because as our brains develop, we look for quick interpretations of events and easy solutions to problems so we don't expend too much energy thinking about what we're doing. Thinking is hard work; our brains consume approximately 20 percent of the body's energy every day. These patterns of behavior and thinking become habits. This makes life easier and conserves energy, but the side effect is that we often make mistakes and poor decisions relying on these habits without realizing it.

Take a moment to look at the illustration below:

Can you find the the mistake?
1 2 3 4 5 6 7 8 9 10

We bet you couldn't find the mistake if you're like most of us. Go back and look at the graphic again and you will see that the first line has a typo in it. Can you find "the the" mistake? The reason you missed that error was "the" was typed twice in a row but your brain was on autopilot as it was impacted by a cognitive bias named Tunnel Vison. This cognitive bias causes your brain to focus on "what it expects to see" and causes you to miss looking at what is really there. Your brain simply assumed that the mistake wasn't in the instructions and started looking elsewhere because it followed old habits. The Tunnel Vision bias is often the reason we overlook things that can impact our ability to gain a sale. This seems so obvious in retrospect that we can't believe we missed it.

Key Things to Remember About the Principles of Adaptive Selling

- There is no "one best" sales method. Top performers know various sales methods and diagnose the selling situation to determine the most appropriate sales methodologies to employ.

- In every sales situation, relationships are almost always the most important factor in winning.

- Every person engaged in a sales situation brings unstated cognitive biases to the interaction that can help, hinder, or prevent a positive outcome.

- An understanding of SOCIAL STYLE and Versatility helps cultivate and nourish relationships and anticipate and address cognitive biases related to decision-making, risk-taking, use of time, and approach to others. Throughout the following chapters of this book, you will learn the keys for putting this to work for you.

• Team-selling situations succeed when team resources are deployed in a socially intelligent way that maximizes core strengths.

• Preparation is key for every meeting and presentation, especially on the "Soft Side" where Social Intelligence is essential to Adaptive Selling success.

• Learning from "Win and Loss Reviews" improves future outcomes.

Adaptive Selling Assessment

TRACOM has been engaged in training, assessing, and selecting sales people and sales managers since the early 1960s. We have worked with professional service firms, high tech firms, financial and banking firms, manufacturers, software providers, consumer goods companies, retailers, pharmaceutical companies, colleges and universities, governmental agencies, and non-profits. Our solutions are used across the globe in over one hundred countries. Our research has uncovered some common challenges faced by sales people and their organizations. Let's review a few of the most critical categories and do a quick diagnosis of where you might want to strengthen your ability to use Adaptive Selling.

Decide for each category of challenges what your strength is and what a development area is. Be honest with yourself so you can gain some insight into what you need to focus on to become a top performer. Circle your strengths and put an X by your development area in each section.

INDIVIDUAL BEHAVIOR CHALLENGES

- A lack of self-awareness and objective feedback about your strengths and weaknesses.

- A tendency to underestimate the importance of relationships and not devote enough time to relationship maintenance and development.

- Not understanding a client's personal preferences and how best to use that understanding to advance the sale and the relationship.

- Selling to others as though selling to oneself. Saying and doing what you would respond to versus what the client wants and needs.

- Poor questioning, listening, and probing skills.

BUSINESS ACUMEN CHALLENGES

- Not doing one's homework! A lack of active curiosity about the client's business, competitors, market environment, and the threats and opportunities faced by clients.

- Assuming clients have not done their homework on available resources for addressing their needs.

- Being product-focused rather than developing compelling

and innovative applications that make a substantial difference to a client's business.

• Not understanding the decision-making process of clients— not knowing who is involved, their roles, and how they influence each other.

• Not adequately preparing for meetings with both clients and with the sales person's internal team.

• Assuming too much.

• Not learning from Wins and Losses.

EMOTIONAL INTELLIGENCE (EQ) Challenges

• Weak people skills for identifying and managing emotions of self and others.

• Failure to demonstrate behaviors linked to empathy—what is often referred to as the "soft-side" of selling.

• Inability to identify and apply behaviors that demonstrate each of the key components of EQ.

RESILENCE AND AGILITY CHALLENGES

• Resistance to change in how to sell in today's rapidly changing marketplaces.

• Lack of understanding of cognitive biases in self and others and how to overcome them.

- Weakness at identifying problems/opportunities and developing innovative solutions.

- Insufficient understanding of how to energize clients around a solution.

- Implementation/application weakness.

How did you do? Do you see these challenges in your organization? Which ones do you think are your greatest opportunities for improvement?

Let's now address these challenges by offering a comprehensive set of skills and applications that can be integrated together to form a powerful and winning strategy to enrich your current skill set.

THE NEED FOR ADAPTIVE SELLING

What Is a Sales Person?

As guest lecturers at several respected universities, the one question we always ask our audiences is which of them plan to go into sales. Most times, no hands go up. When a follow-up question is asked as to their impressions of sales people, the results aren't too surprising. Their impressions are that sales people are mostly shallow and insincere and that selling is not a truly honorable profession. Selling is often seen as a manipulative and pressure-filled process designed to get someone to buy regardless of whether or not they want or need to buy.

Certainly, there are sales people who are only interested in making the sale for their personal interest. Great sales people, however, are quite the opposite.

One of the things that most of us have learned is that everyone is in sales, whether they realize it or not. Senior executives often take the position that dealing with customers is a key responsibility for every employee—that is selling.

"I have always said that everyone is in sales. Maybe you don't hold the title of salesperson, but if the business you are in requires you to deal with people, you, my friend, are in sales." [3]
—Zig Ziglar

So what it is that people do when they sell? The following sales continuum will begin to answer that question. It starts with Basic Product Selling on the left side and then moves through various other methodologies to Complex Selling on the right side.

Sales people using the Product Selling methodology talk about the features of their product or solution and the credibility of their organization. This approach is fine for product selling to mass markets. Listen to an Apple announcement of a new product. It's all about faster speeds, bigger screens, better cameras, and improved screen resolution and so on. This is suitable for what they are selling but doesn't work very well for companies selling large, expensive products or solutions.

In this situation, a commonly relied on sales method is one where the sales or business development team takes the time to understand client needs and then demonstrates how their solution can fulfill those needs. They start by questioning and probing before offering solutions. These sales people are like good doctors who don't prescribe treatments until after an examination. A weakness with these methods is that it is mostly used to convince a buyer that the standard or slightly tailored solution the sales person represents meets their needs as opposed to providing a client-centric tailored/custom solution.

Sales people dealing with complex sales need to use to a combination of sales methods to create value for their clients. The key to being able to do this is using Adaptive Selling skills to select and modify the strategy most appropriate for the buyers so that one can win on a consistent basis.

Research by CSO Insights published in 2017 found that quota achievement overall dropped to 53 percent of sales people for 2016. This adaptive approach is significantly more effective in gaining major wins and resulting in as many at 69.8 percent of sales people meeting or exceeding quotas, nearly 17 points higher than average.[4] These sales professionals research and learn the challenges and opportunities their clients are confronting, even those the client is

SALES EFFECTIVENESS CONTINUUM

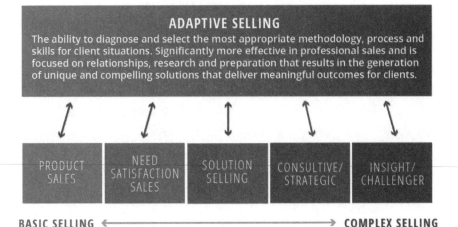

ADAPTIVE SELLING
The ability to diagnose and select the most appropriate methodology, process and skills for client situations. Significantly more effective in professional sales and is focused on relationships, research and preparation that results in the generation of unique and compelling solutions that deliver meaningful outcomes for clients.

| PRODUCT SALES | NEED SATISFACTION SALES | SOLUTION SELLING | CONSULTIVE/ STRATEGIC | INSIGHT/ CHALLENGER |

BASIC SELLING ←————————————————————————→ COMPLEX SELLING

Product Sales approaches are fine for commodity and mass market selling and focus on product features and benefits.

Need-Satisfaction Sales are more consultative and relationship focused but tend to offer standard or slightly tailored solutions as meeting client needs revealed through discussions.

Solution Selling methods focus on customer pains and needs, and collaboratively building a solution to address them. Less focus on what product does and more on how it can solve an issue.

Consultative/Strategic Selling methods focus on using strategic questioning skills with a customer about their most pressing business issues, show value and uniqueness, and having processes to identify decision makers and influencers and sales probabilities.

Insight/Challenger approaches advocates challenging the buyer's perception of their problems, uncovering needs that they don't know they have and/or sharing new ideas for improving their business.

not aware of! Adaptive sales people look for unique ways that resources can be combined to create a high-value outcome that their client has not been able to uncover for themselves. They use their relationship skills to help drive a win for their clients and increase the value of their relationships. All of this builds on a foundation of trust created between the client and the salesperson as a result of their "soft-skills."

Importance of Relationships to Mastering Adaptive Selling

"We have done a lot of research to find out why we win. We found out that there are a lot of criteria clients use to decide who to work with, but there are four that stood out more than anything else. Technical capability is one because, if you can't do the job, clearly you're not going to be considered. The second one is business case. It's not just price but rather, for the fees I'm paying, am I getting the value I'm expecting. More important, though, is the client's view of the team: specifically, does the team look joined up and work well together? Finally, and most important, is cultural fit, by which the client assesses how well we will work together. If we can't work well together, people get disengaged, everything starts taking longer, margins go down, costs go up...It's a nightmare. I think that kind of brought me back to the fact that actually it's all about Versatility. Are you able to flex your style to make it comfortable for the client to work with you? So when we are pursuing an opportunity, we often look at the SOCIAL STYLE and Versatility of the individual team members and try to assess that of the key influencers and we tailor our proposals."

— Tracy Embo
Associate Director, EY UK

The evidence from many Win-Loss Reviews after significant deals shows that the quality of relationships is the most important of all buying factors. For example, if you have great relationships, then the client will feel comfortable and will even want to tell you where you are weak and where you are strong. The client will be willing to listen to your insights into their business and their problems and trust you to create a powerful and innovative solution that will make a positive difference.

While some current articles and books dispute the importance of relationships, many professionals strongly disagree. Research does not bear out this lack of importance of relationships to success as reflected in the LinkedIn research around the importance of trust for decision makers.

Win-Loss Reviews don't directly discuss the key role of the relationship, but it has been found that buyers buy emotionally but then rationalize their decision. The rational explanation rarely includes the relationship. Typically, Win-Loss Reviews only deconstruct the rational side of the decision; further probing is needed to determine the quality and importance of relationships to a successful outcome.

A senior Deal Coach who uses Adaptive Selling worked with a senior account team responsible for the relationship with a major telecom equipment supplier. One of the account teams with whom this coach applied Adaptive Selling generated $2 billion in revenue from their client. They strongly felt that the quality of their relationships was the most important factor in their success. This has been true in most sales successes.

Great sales people master how to build and nourish better relationships. They know that they are not going to be truly successful if this is not accomplished on a consistent basis. What is needed is a systematic way of cultivating and nourishing powerful relationships

> *"And the only way that I can drive the type of initiatives that I do in my job is to build a large, powerful network and have really strong relationships. That takes the ability to be versatile and adaptable, because nothing works without a trusting relationship!"*
>
> **— Nancy Kopp:** EY Americas

that is simple and easy to put into practice.

Research shows that the following are the primary elements of a relationship:

- **Trust** is the first thing that everyone will bring up. But trust is an outcome of engaging in the skills and behaviors integral to Adaptive Selling.

- **Likability** can make it easier to have a meaningful relationship with people yet it is still possible to have a positive outcome when people don't like us but respect us. The key is having the skills to work with differences.

- **Commonalities** are the anchor for many relationships. For example, we may have a relationship because we went to school together or have the same hobbies. If these don't exist, great sales people develop commonalities around the client's business and their challenges.

- **Reliability, Credibility, Loyalty,** and **Consistency** fuel a better relationship.

- **Responsiveness** and **Perseverance**, such as getting back to people on a timely basis with emails and voice messages, means a lot to most of us. So does not giving up when delays and changes occur. Do what you say you will do and do it in a timely manner so you will become a key partner for your client.

• **Transparency** and **Openness** strengthen relationships.

• Being seen as **Helpful** builds loyalty and trust.

• Finally, relationships can be enhanced with true **Empathic** and **EQ** skills where compassion is shown for the other person's feelings.

Throughout our careers, we have come to appreciate more and more the concept of connecting with people. This is the point where we see that we have started a relationship. Sometimes it happens quickly, other times it may take a while, and sometimes we don't achieve it at all. Relationship masters often try to quickly connect around commonalties. Try it! You have a lot to win.

Typical Deal-Flow Stages, Best Practices, and Skills

"Many of the sales processes and methods in the market today are fine and they can work. What they typically do not address is EQ, the softer set of selling skills that are required to be consistently successful in sales. And that comes at you from different dimensions. It's not just the client interactions. It's the pursuit team that you build on the selling side. It's the delivery leadership team and how they mirror the client from a SOCIAL STYLE standpoint, demographically, and from an organization-accountability perspective."

— John Maguire
Senior Vice President, Chief Sales Officer—Cognizant

The Adaptive Selling Model

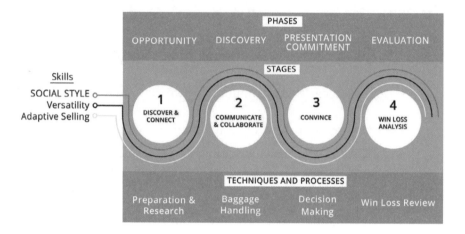

The **Opportunities** Phase comes from existing clients, alumni clients, and potential clients. They may be sole source or competitive.

Opportunities are where we enter into the **"Discover and Connect"** stage where we better understand the people and more about the opportunity. We strive to connect with the people involved so we develop and nurture a relationship.

The next stage is **"Communicate and Collaborate"** which is in the Discovery Phase. Here is where we are meeting with the client and starting to collaborate on a solution.

In the Presentation and Commitment Phase, we then enter the **"Convince"** stage, where we are proposing and presenting solutions to the decision makers. If we follow the proven best practices and skills in this book, then we are far more likely to win.

Finally, in the Evaluation Phase we need to learn what we did well and what we can improve on through the **"Win-Loss"** stage.

Throughout this process flow, top sales people use their skills at managing behavioral differences and interpersonal tensions, building mutually productive relationships, and overcoming cognitive biases. These are key for being able to apply Adaptive Selling and selecting the best sales approach and customizing it to the client.

Skills and Best Practices

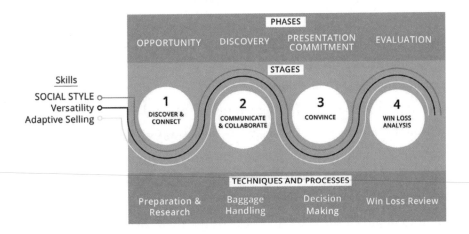

The skills and best practices for Adaptive Selling are shown as weaving themselves throughout the entire sales process. In addition, key applications that drive the effectiveness of Adaptive Selling are shown as building blocks with the process.

Adaptive Selling heavily stresses the critical importance of relationships. Techniques for connecting, which is the first step for building a relationship, and then the development and nurturing of relationships is what it is about.

SOCIAL STYLE underpins every stage of a deal. SOCIAL

STYLE is an empirically researched behavioral model that shows who we are, the behavioral styles of those we deal with, and guides us on how to better understand and deal with each other.

Versatility is the extent to which others perceive us as using our Style appropriately with them. It is a measure of three key dimensions: Presentation, Competence, and Feedback. How we communicate, use language, listen and respond, show empathy, display optimism, persevere through difficulties, meet deadlines, help others achieve their goals, demonstrate conscientiousness, and meet our goals are all elements of these dynamic dimensions. The good news is Versatility is changeable. We can improve it, whereas our Style has a low probability of changing. So don't try to change your Style; learn how to use it with Versatility to succeed across a wide range of audiences.

Adaptive Selling is the ability to apply a variety of sales approaches based on doing one's research and developing a full understanding before offering solutions. **SOCIAL STYLE** is a foundational skill for being able to do this. **Baggage Handling** is an empathetic technique for connecting with others by understanding and acknowledging their feelings. **Decision Mapping** helps one understand how decisions are made, who makes them, and how to plan to deploy resources that best fit the map. **Research** and adequate **Preparation** are essential to every step of a deal. Ultimately, **Win-Loss Analysis** is where we learn what we did well and what we did poorly from the mouths of our clients.

Most companies want to improve their overall sales effectiveness. Many seem to think that their problem is in not having a sales process that monitors the stages of a deal as shown above. For sure, it is good to have a process which can track the progress of individual deals and also see how many deals are at each stage. Having a sales process also gives people a common language and allows them to forecast better. For example, discovering that sales should be winning or closing 60 percent of deals in the "Convince" stage can help keep a continuous flow of sales.

But be careful of making the process too complicated or burdensome for everyone.

Even more important than having a common sales process is having institutionalized best practices and skills like those Adaptive Selling focuses on.

Looking at this from another perspective, organizations might have fine sales processes but also have poor sales skills, such as lack of research and market knowledge, little questioning and probing and planning for meetings, combined with little use of best practices, such as rehearsals or properly organizing presentations. The result of this is poor sales execution.

On the other hand, organizations with great sales skills that use the best practices mentioned above may do very well even if there is no formalized sales process. In summary, develop the skills and best practices first, but having a good sales process is also useful.

USING SOCIAL STYLE TO BUILD AND NURTURE RELATIONSHIPS IS AT THE HEART OF ADAPTIVE SELLING

What Exactly is SOCIAL STYLE?

SOCIAL STYLE provides a systematic way of understanding how to build and nourish productive relationships which are essential to Adaptive Selling. The model shows the way people are different in their behaviors, what creates negative and positive tension for them, how they use time and make decisions, and how they like to be treated when interacting. It is foundational to effectively build rapport, gain trust, and communicate for mutual gain.

> "SOCIAL STYLE is part of the Cognizant way to sell. It's embedded into the way we sell. We use different outside firms and former CXOs in our sales instruction. We make sure everybody understands SOCIAL STYLE and references back to it and how to use it. It is a fully integrated part of what we do; it's in our CRM system, and has become part of the dialogue at Cognizant."
>
> **— John Maguire**
> **Senior Vice President, Chief Sales Officer—Cognizant**

To understand the importance of SOCIAL STYLE, it is necessary to discover the cognitive biases that distort how we Think, Act, and React to the world around us, and how these impact our performance. Knowing your SOCIAL STYLE and Versatility helps you overcome these unconscious biases and increases your ability to build trusting and high-performing relationships. Let's look deeper into these hidden barriers to performance.

We know that all people are affected by cognitive biases. Why? Because as our brains develop, we look for quick interpretations of events and easy solutions to problems so we don't have to expend too much energy thinking about what we're doing. As mentioned earlier, these patterns of behavior and thinking become habits. Thinking is hard work; our brains consume approximately 20 percent of the body's energy every day. Habits make life easier and conserve energy, but the side effect is that we often make mistakes and poor decisions without realizing it.

Cognitive biases evolved for good reasons. They helped us to process information quickly, meet basic needs, and survive in hostile environments. However, in the modern world, these biases come with costs. When we *should* be expending effort analyzing situations to make sure that we are making sound decisions, our brains trick us into taking the convenient path.

When communicating and working with others such as in sales, we are affected by the *Self-Evaluation Bias*. This bias influences how we see ourselves and how we interpret others' behavior. First, it causes us to see ourselves inaccurately, meaning we don't have very good self-awareness of how we come across to others. In other words, when we look in the mirror we may see someone younger and better-looking, and this generalizes to all sorts of other areas, such as our job performance, creative ability, and skill at communicating. How often are you surprised by the sound of your own voice when you listen to a when you listen to a recording of yourself talking? If you're like most people, you are surprised to realize that is how you sound to others. This is another common example of how our Self-Perception differs from reality. More importantly, this bias causes us to misinterpret the actions of others; when someone fails to do what we expect or does something we don't agree with, we attribute it to their personality or character rather than circumstances or simple behavioral style differences. Research shows that the majority of people view themselves differently than how they are seen by others, yet it is the perception of others that drives how they respond to someone.

In sales, this combination of poor self-awareness and misunderstanding of others creates problems because people don't recognize one another's preferences for getting things done. We communicate and interact in ways that reflect our own needs without accounting for others' needs and preferences. Then, when our clients or colleagues don't respond in ways we expect, we hold it against them which leads to ongoing misunderstandings and deterioration of relationships. Breaking this bias is as simple as learning about different behavioral styles and how people prefer to communicate and perform their work. With this knowledge, we can adapt how we communicate and work with others, and these simple changes lead to greater personal effectiveness and higher sales performance. We can become aware of our own behaviors and how they are perceived by others through feedback from other people. This can help us recognize how our behavior impedes our performance and effectiveness, particularly during stressful times of change. We can also learn how to recognize the behavioral styles of others and how to communicate with them in ways that lead to understanding and acceptance. In sales, this helps one to more effectively navigate through large-scale challenges and change.

We spend a large percentage of our lives at work, and this means that the relationships we develop there are critical, not only to our personal and organizational effectiveness, but to our well-being. The importance of developing deep, meaningful relationships has been widely studied and is affected by our ability to empathize with others.

Unfortunately, our skill at empathy is frequently undermined by the *Transparency Bias*, which causes us to believe that others accurately recognize *our* emotional state, and also to overestimate how accurately we understand *others'* emotional states. In other words, we think we're open books when we aren't, and we believe that others are easy to read when they're not. It's a cognitive and emotional double whammy. This bias gets in the way when we want to develop meaningful relationships with clients and within the team. We make assumptions about others, believing they understand what is going on in our minds and that they can detect our emotions. Essentially, we believe people think like us and therefore we treat them as if they are just like us, experiencing the same beliefs and emotions. Likewise, we think we recognize and understand others' emotions, but we're often wrong, misinterpreting others' signals. When a co-worker is upset about something, we often fail to recognize this and treat them as if nothing has happened, discounting their feelings and unintentionally damaging the relationship.

To break this bias, people can learn strategies to enhance their Versatility or Emotional intelligence (EQ). Simple behavior change, such as active listening and paying closer attention to people's body language and facial expressions, can go a long way toward more accurate understanding of others.

Conversely, developing better self-awareness is critical for overcoming the Transparency Bias. This can be achieved by using an assessment of your emotional triggers to learn about the things that cause you to feel stressed, frustrated, or angry. This simple act has been shown to lead to greater emotional understanding and self-control during difficult times. Greater self-insight is also achieved by getting regular feedback on strengths and weaknesses. Hard as it often is to get feedback, it's critical for overcoming this bias and developing better relationships. Connecting better with others helps work performance and has been identified as one of the most critical skills for the future.

As we move into the era of automation and disruption in the world of sales and buying, profound change is going to happen, and change causes stress for people. Research has shown that people don't easily or quickly recover from setbacks, and as people's work lives are fundamentally changed by automation and disruption, we are going to experience large numbers of people whose lives are negatively affected. Organizations need to be Agile, but they also need sales people who are Resilient in the face of massive change.

Resilience is the capacity to adapt to change, adversity, and stress in a way that allows people to bounce back, but also to bounce forward—to grow and improve. Our ability to recover and move forward during change is affected as we saw earlier by the *Negativity Bias*, which causes us to focus on the "bad" more than the "good." The Negativity Bias evolved to help us survive dangers in our environment—wild animals, poisonous food, and severe weather were just some of the threats that needed to be avoided. In the modern world, the fight/flight/freeze response is more often triggered by perceived threats to our psychological safety, such as feeling powerless in the face of change. This bias affects our beliefs, attitudes, and responses to change and holds us back from coping with difficulties, and potentially from being able to move forward in a way that leads to personal growth and opportunity.

The Negativity Bias is broken by a number of behavioral

strategies that help people build different areas of Resilience, such as realistic optimism, problem solving, self-composure in the face of change, and social support to buffer against hard times. Fundamentally, people learn to recognize the automatic thoughts that all people have in reaction to stressful events. These automatic thoughts are almost always negative, perceiving events as threats. For example, when a change is announced at a major client, many sales people will invent a catastrophe for themselves, believing that the worst possible outcome is the most likely. This, in turn, affects their ability to be proactive and ensure that the change benefits them. Understanding this bias and adopting strategies to help build personal Resilience will help organizations successfully navigate large-scale change in the future.

A key tool for overcoming these cognitive biases is the SOCIAL STYLE Model which was originally developed by Dr. David Merrill and Roger Reid who were founders of what is now known as the TRACOM Corporation. They undertook a major empirical research project to determine what could predict success in sales and management. Much of their original research was focused on the education, insurance, and financial services industries and led to the development of an assessment for predicting success. Dr. Merrill built a highly successful selection and assessment business that he later expanded into training. Today SOCIAL STYLE is used in over 100 countries to help managers, salespeople, and professionals achieve high performance. TRACOM has continued to research and evolve the SOCIAL STYLE Assessment and Profile Report to maintain its relevance. It has expanded the tool with more applications and skills for putting it to work in today's global workplace. The Profile is normed so that the results of measuring its three key components are relevant in every part of the world. The measuring of a person's Style through the SOCIAL STYLE Multi-Rater

Assessment is critical for helping overcome major cognitive biases.

At its most basic level, the SOCIAL STYLE Model has three independent dimensions:

1. Assertiveness

2. Responsiveness

3. Versatility

Assertiveness and Responsiveness are behavioral dimensions measured by the frequency of the behaviors associated with each dimension being used in interactions with others. Versatility is a measure of how others perceive the appropriateness with which someone uses their behavior when interacting with them.

Assertiveness is the horizontal axis of the four-quadrant model formed by intersecting the two independent behavioral dimensions of SOCIAL STYLE. People on the right-hand side demonstrate a faster pace and would be generally perceived as being more telling or directing in how they assert themselves. They tell more, take risks, make declarative statements, and are decisive. For example, they will make a decision in a meeting. An important thing to know about people on the right side is that they will initiate actions. This means taking ideas to them can move things forward.

ASSERTIVENESS

ASKS ←——————————→ TELLS

Risk Avoiders   Risk Takers
Slower Decisions   Quick Decisions
Avoid Imposing   Initiators

People on the left-hand side of the model assert themselves by asking questions. They seek to minimize risk, take more time to make decisions, and avoid imposing their ideas on others. They often make conditional statements like, "it depends." Don't expect them to make decisions in meetings. To move ideas forward with them you will need to provide data or assurances and allow time for processing.

Responsiveness or Emotiveness provides the vertical axis of the SOCIAL STYLE Model. This measures how we control or display emotions. People at the Top or North end of the model are difficult to read: don't play poker with them. Folks on the other end are just the opposite.

RESPONSIVENESS

CONTROLS EMOTIONS
Harder to Read
Structured Use of Time
Task Oriented

DISPLAYS EMOTIONS
Easier to Read
Unstructured Use of Time
Relationship Oriented

North-Enders in the Emote part of the model are impersonal, less social, communicate cautiously or only when they feel a need to do so, and are more task oriented. Get down to business with them more quickly and have an agenda. They respond well to fact-based meetings.

South-Enders show their feelings and are more social, communicate openly, share personal information, and are less task-oriented. They are more open, feeling-oriented, and like non-structured meetings and free flowing conversations.

These two independent dimensions of behavior can be combined to form a very useful four-quadrant model for helping understand one's own behavioral preferences as well as those of others. This information can then be used to help build the most productive and successful relationships and avoid the common missteps most people make when interacting with others who have different ways of using time, interacting, and making decisions. Being able to work with others whose preferences are different from our own is what distinguishes highly successful sales professionals.

The SOCIAL STYLE Model

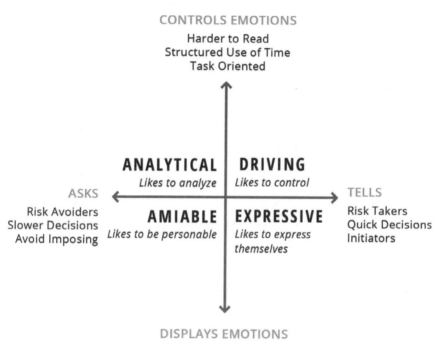

CONTROLS EMOTIONS
Harder to Read
Structured Use of Time
Task Oriented

ANALYTICAL | **DRIVING**
Likes to analyze | *Likes to control*

ASKS

Risk Avoiders
Slower Decisions
Avoid Imposing

AMIABLE | **EXPRESSIVE**
Likes to be personable | *Likes to express themselves*

TELLS

Risk Takers
Quick Decisions
Initiators

DISPLAYS EMOTIONS
Easier to Read
Unstructured Use of Time
Relationship Oriented

Meet the Four SOCIAL STYLEs

> "Of all the sales tools and methodologies that we've deployed, Style is the one that's landed the most effectively. It's interesting and easy to use. I see Style being used in our organization around the world. We see TRACOM as clearly being advantageous in a business development setting, but we see it as a much broader tool than that."
>
> **— Peter Matthews:** Senior Partner

Top sales people know how to use observable behavior to quickly identify another person's preferences and use that knowledge to make informed choices to keep the interaction as comfortable and productive as possible. This ability to moderate one's behavior is called Versatility and is gained when a person has a proven approach for classifying behaviors and choosing alternative responses while managing their cognitive biases. An easy to apply framework for overcoming distortions in how one Thinks, Acts, and Reacts due to their cognitive biases is TRACOM's proprietary SOCIAL STYLE Model. Style evolved out of TRACOM's empirical research on the key differentiators of success in sales and management. Ongoing studies continue to show that sales people who apply the Model in their careers have been proven to be more successful in generating sales and gaining trust. They are better communicators, more effective in leadership roles, and build better customer and team relationships than others. And this success has been shown to be universal regardless of what part of the globe one calls home.

Let's begin with a brief review of the four Styles—Analytical, Driving, Expressive, and Amiable—before exploring how to use the characteristics of each Style to select the behaviors that have the highest chance of success.

Basic Description of the Analytical Style

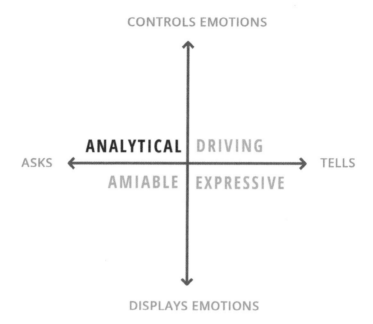

People with an Analytical Style emote less and ask more than they tell. They like data and processes. They are slower paced and avoid risks. They like agendas and structured conversations. They are likely to be less social and prefer to work independently. They make conditional statements such as, "It depends," when asked questions.

Analytical Style people like to see all of the data. If shown a spreadsheet, watch them lower their heads. They likely will tune everything out while doing this.

They look at things historically. ***Their basic need is "to be right."*** This isn't about ego; it is about making correct decisions based on facts and figures that they believe to hold up historically and fit within their principles and processes. They want quality solutions—for example, so that the bridges they design don't fall down!

Another good word for colleagues with an Analytical Style is "double-clickers." When given a fact, they probe or double-click to learn more. Don't present shoddy data to an Analytical Style; it can cost their trust and increase their skepticism.

Their value to the organization is that they provide quality and durability. They probe, look at things from different angles, and take their time before making decisions. We often find that when there is a problematic engagement, there were not enough Analytical-Style hands on deck.

While there are Analytical Styles in all industries and in all roles, a significant percentage of engineers, accountants, and IT types live in this quadrant. Examples of the Analytical Style are President Barack Obama and Katherine Coleman Johnson, famous for her work at NASA and subject of the movie *Hidden Figures*.

> *"If you're walking down the right path and you're willing to keep walking, eventually you'll make progress."*
>
> —Barack Obama, 44th President of the United States

> *"Let me do it. You tell me when you want it and where you want it to land and I'll do it backwards and tell you when to take off."*
>
> —Katherine Coleman Johnson, Mathematician whose calculations of orbital mechanics as a NASA employee were critical to the success of the first and subsequent U.S. manned spaceflights.

Basic Description of the Driving Style

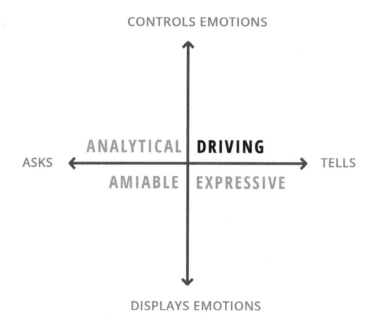

The Driving Style emotes less and tells more than asks. They like facts and data but not as comprehensively as the Analytical Style does. To explain, they will take one piece of data and drill down to test; however, they generally don't want to drill down with all of the data. They want to move. They are fact-based only to the extent they are able to determine options for action. Their time frame is today.

Examples of the Driving Style are Steve Jobs, the former CEO at Apple, who turned the company around in the mid-nineties and the Chancellor of Germany, Angela Merkel.

> *"It's not about charisma and personality; it's about results and products…"*
>
> —Steve Jobs, Apple, Inc.

Mr. Jobs had no taste for moving slowly and avoiding risks.

"The question is not whether we are able to change but whether we are changing fast enough."

—Angela Merkel, Chancellor of Germany

Driving Style individuals like to get down to business. They will ask challenging questions, so be prepared for them. Impatience is one of their telling characteristics. Furthermore, they like to be in control.

The basic need of the Driving Style is to achieve results, the quicker the better. They are risk-takers. The value of Driving Style individuals is that they get things done, on time and within budget although there may be some resentment from others regarding their approach.

Some mistakenly believe that most CEOs are the Driving Style or should be. There certainly are a lot of CEOs who are the Driving Style, but CEOs come in all Styles. In general, the Driving Style is good for project managers and implementers because of their focus on results.

On one project undertaken by TRACOM, we would meet with the sponsoring executive weekly to discuss the project. At the end of each meeting, she had an index card on her desk where she would write to-dos for us and herself.

You are guessing that she started meetings by pulling this card and checking results and you are right!

The Driving Style is big on to-do lists.

Basic Description of the Expressive Style

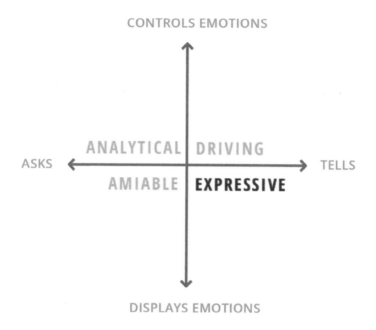

The Expressive Style is on the right bottom of the model. People with this Style have high energy, share emotions easily, and tell more than they ask. While competitive, they enjoy being around people and are very approachable. Their time frame is the future. Typically, they are the innovators and energizers in organizations. They are risk takers.

They can be unstructured in their conversations and often mix in humor, not always appropriately. They readily state their opinions. Data diving can be a chore for them.

Their need is for personal approval and recognition. To achieve this, they do creative things that are admired and showcased to others. Expressive Style colleagues bring new ideas, fun, excitement, and creativity to an organization.

Examples of the Expressive Style are Elon Musk, the CEO at

Tesla, SpaceX, and Neuralink, and co-founder of PayPal, Richard Branson, CEO of Virgin Group, and President Bill Clinton.

> *"If you get up in the morning and think the future is going to be better, it is a bright day. Otherwise, it's not."*
>
> —Elon Musk, Tesla and SpaceX

> *"If somebody offers you an amazing opportunity but you are not sure you can do it, say yes—then learn how to do it later!"*
>
> —Richard Branson, Virgin Group

Expressive-Style people like to create and generate excitement, fun, and impact the future. They will put forward their ideas readily and may not be very organized in how they do it, so be prepared for them. Impatience is one of their telling characteristics especially if things get bogged down in details. While friendly, casual, and approachable, the Expressive Style likes to win. They are competitive and focused on the big picture.

The basic need of the Expressive Style is approval or recognition of their ideas and the value they provide to the organization or group. They are risk-takers but don't focus on the details. They are much more intuitive. The value of Expressive-Style individuals is that they get things moving with excitement and energy. They are creative and like to involve others. However, they are undisciplined in how they use time and creative with any facts so that they can advance their ideas. Their spontaneity and easy sharing of feelings and opinions can create discomfort and resentment in others, especially those who are more Controlled Responsive.

The Expressive Style can be the most common SOCIAL STYLE in sales organizations. In fact, two of the sales-oriented companies where TRACOM has worked were composed mainly of people with an Expressive Style. Another sector containing many people of this SOCIAL STYLE is the legal profession; recent data analysis at TRACOM have shown more attorneys in this quadrant than previously thought. There is a listing of Styles by industry in the Appendix.

Basic Description of the Amiable Style

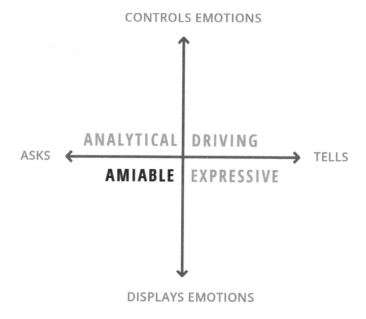

The Amiable Style is on the bottom left of the model. People with this Style are open to others, casual, share emotions, and ask more than they tell. They enjoy being involved with others and are very approachable. Their time frame is the present, and they are not very disciplined in how they use time. In groups, they are focused on gaining consensus and making sure everyone is heard. They are the most people-oriented style.

They can be unstructured in their conversations and focus on opinions and stories more than facts and data. Because they don't want to create any difficulties with others, they frequently fail to state their opinions and positions. They can also come across as having lower energy than the more Tell Assertive Styles. Data is not nearly as important for them as are relationships.

Their need is for personal security. To achieve this, they tend to focus on building relationships with a wide range of people. Amiable-Style colleagues bring consideration, engagement and sensitivity to organizations. People with an Amiable Style can be the glue that holds organizations together by promoting harmony and reason.

The Amiable Style is sensitive to change management issues in that they often don't like massive change. They are risk averse, especially toward risks that involve people. They like proven processes, products, and solutions.

Examples of the Amiable Style are Oprah Winfrey and former President George H.W. Bush.

> *"The reason I so rarely break promises to other people? It breaks trust. Without trust, there's no relationship."*
>
> —Oprah Winfrey, American media proprietor, talk show host, actress, producer, and philanthropist

> *"America is never wholly herself unless she is engaged in high moral principle. We as a people have such a purpose today. It is to make kinder the face of the nation and gentler the face of the world."*
>
> —George H.W. Bush, 41st President of the United States

People with the Amiable Style are naturally the strongest Style at building relationships. You will see many healthcare and human resources professionals and educators here.

A word of caution here is necessary. Research shows there is "No Best Style!" All Styles succeed as well as fail. All Styles exist in all organizations and at all levels. Style does not determine success. The key is how someone uses their Style.

Things to Remember about the Needs by Style When Selling

The Needs of the Analytical Style

First, let's understand that Analytical Style people are skeptical and don't like to be sold. The Analytical Style wants to be Right. Here are some of their needs:

• Data/Evidence—Analytical Style clients like to analyze, so give them data/evidence. Don't try to condense the numbers for them. Instead, offer them everything.

• Transparency—they want to see and understand everything. Don't hide anything. Show them estimates and work plans, for example.

• Understanding—take the time to understand everything you can about where they are, what problems they have, and what they see as the challenges. Think of this as "double-clicking the double clickers."

• Time to consider—don't pressure someone with an Analytical Style for quick decisions. For example, they don't like to make decisions in meetings where they haven't seen the data before.

• Mitigate the risks that they see.

• Try to be as accurate as possible, but don't claim that what you have is perfect.

• Don't shoot from the hip with this Style. If you don't know, don't fake it. Tell them you will find out and get back to them.

• Don't deal in generalities and only big picture. Get into specifics and details.

• Let them know they will not have to make an immediate decision.

The Needs of the Driving Style

Remember that the Driving Style wants Results, the quicker the better. Here are some of their other needs:

• Avoid overgeneralizing—they like to deal with peers and gurus.

• Demonstrate capabilities—they want to work with people who can deliver results.

• Be businesslike and candid—the Driving Style likes to be challenged.

• Be efficient—they will appreciate you saving them time, and not wasting time with topics they don't consider important.

• Respect their time—put people with relevant experience in front of them.

• Get to business quickly—don't worry about warming up with personal discussions unless they initiate one. Even then, get to business soon.

• Quick wins are compelling for them.

• The Driving Style likes to be in control or at least have input. Give them the chance to make the decision.

• They want facts and data, but only in brief form.

• Don't give them a single alternative to making a decision— they want options.

The Needs of the Expressive Style

People with an Expressive Style want to be recognized and admired for their creativity, innovation, and energy. They also need:

• Support—they like those who can enable their visions.

• Approval from others—don't compete with them for recognition or creativity.

• Respect—they like to be seen as thought leaders.

• Being considered important—they respond well to attention and nourishment especially from senior executives.

• To share—give them time to talk about what's important to

them, even if it is not specifically tied to the purpose of the meeting.

• Don't want to be left out—where possible try to put the Expressive Style on key committees or oversight boards and keep them in the loop on issues.

• Association with others they consider important—let them know which other people/organizations that they admire have done business with you.

• Can perceive outside experts as competitors or threats.

The Needs of the Amiable Style

Remember that the Amiable Style wants to have positive relationships. In addition, they need:

• Socialization—take time to get to know them on a personal level.

• Safety—seek to minimize risks for them.

• Time to share—don't try to over-structure meetings.

• Considered decisions—use a slower pace in taking actions or making a decision.

• Empathy—make the effort to share feelings and build personal trust.

• People-orientation—don't appreciate someone who overdoes facts and logic to the exclusion of people.

• Time to decide—don't expect a quick decision and don't attempt to pressure them.

• Engagement—they want others involved in actions and decisions.

• Consensus—they are supportive of any action or decision that involves others and gains their approval.

• Equality—they don't seek power over others and they don't appreciate those who do.

• Reassurance—they would like to know that similar projects have successfully been done many times before.

What Happens Under Stress

When trying to figure out your own behavioral style, consider how you behave under high tension:

• Do you want to take over, take control, and become autocratic? If so, then you are most likely in the Driving Style quadrant.

• Do you let your emotions be known or attack others, sometimes in a personal way? Then you probably have an Expressive Style.

• Do you prefer to not commit, create alone-time in order to think, and analyze data or the situation? If so, then you likely have an Analytical Style.

• Do you want to preserve harmony such that you will go along with what the majority wants even if you don't agree? Then you probably are an Amiable Style.

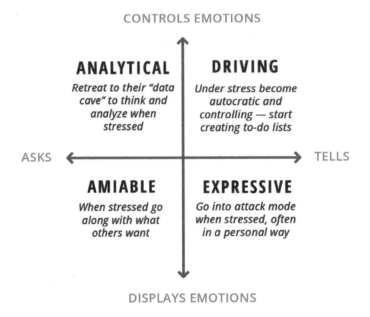

CONTROLS EMOTIONS

ANALYTICAL
Retreat to their "data cave" to think and analyze when stressed

DRIVING
Under stress become autocratic and controlling — start creating to-do lists

ASKS ⟵   ⟶ TELLS

AMIABLE
When stressed go along with what others want

EXPRESSIVE
Go into attack mode when stressed, often in a personal way

DISPLAYS EMOTIONS

How To Determine a Person's SOCIAL SYLE

The most accurate way to know someone else's SOCIAL STYLE is to have them take TRACOM's multi-rater assessment, which measures a person's SOCIAL STYLE as determined by others and compared against others in their country or region. An alternative is to use TRACOM's STYLE Estimator which is included in the SOCIAL STYLE Navigator application. While these approaches will get you the information you need, they may not be practical, especially in situations where you meet someone for the first time during a sales call.

The most frequently used approach to determine a person's Style is observation. It is important never to simply guess a person's

SOCIAL STYLE, as this guess may be wrong. Too often people guess someone's Style by focusing on their job title or their occupation. It is important to understand that all Styles succeed and all Styles are at all levels and types of occupations.

The typical behaviors explained in the previous section can help with sound identification of someone's Style. Let's look at how to use the dimensions of the SOCIAL STYLE Model to estimate a person's Style.

The best way is to be systematic. *First, look at Assertiveness* —the horizontal axis of the model. Start with the question: "Does the person have high or low energy?" This seems to work most of the time. Then ask yourself: "Is the person decisive?" Then, "Do they make declarative or conditional statements? People on the right (the Driving Style and Expressive Style) make declarative statements, have high energy, are fast-paced and are decisive. Left siders (Analytical and Amiable Styles) make conditional statements, such as the classic: "It depends," have a lower display of energy, move at a slower pace, and are hesitant to make decisions without having time to consider the issue.

ASKS ◄───────────────────────► TELLS
Risk Avoiders   Risk Takers
Slower Decisions   Quick Decisions
Avoid Imposing   Initiators

If the answers to these questions indicate a right-sided person, they are either a Driving or Expressive Style. And this tells you a lot about what to expect from them and how to work with them most productively.

Emotiveness or Responsiveness

RESPONSIVENESS

CONTROLS EMOTIONS
Harder to Read
Structured Use of Time
Task Oriented

DISPLAYS EMOTIONS
Easier to Read
Unstructured Use of Time
Relationship Oriented

This dimension of Responsiveness or Emotiveness is a bit harder to determine compared to Assertiveness. Here are some of the questions that can assist in determining where someone falls on this dimension. "Does this person readily show their emotions—can you read them?" "Are they structured and task-oriented?" "Are they less social or more social?"

If the answers indicate that the person is hard to read, less social, and task oriented, then the person has either an Analytical or

Driving Style. If they are easy to read, very social, and people-oriented, then the person is either an Expressive or Amiable Style.

Also think about how the person acts under stress as described earlier; actions under stress can be very telling, as well as how they act in meetings.

Whatever the answers to these questions might be, proceed with the subsequent list of follow-up questions.

Confirming Questions for Each SOCIAL STYLE

CONFIRMING QUESTIONS
FOR EACH SOCIAL STYLE

ANALYTICAL
• Do they like all data?
• Do they take time to make decisions?
• Are they less social and reserved?

DRIVING
• Do they seem impatient and task-oriented?
• Are they challenging?
• Do they have direct eye contact?

AMIABLE
• Are they warm and inviting?
• Do they seem agreeable?
• Do they share personal information?
• Do they hesitate to make decision on their own?

EXPRESSIVE
• Do they talk a lot?
• Are they opinionated?
• Did they mix in humor or stories?
• Do they lose track of time?
• Do they have direct eye contact?

GETTING THROUGH TO CLIENTS AND PROSPECTS BASED ON THEIR SOCIAL STYLE PREFERENCES

Applications of the SOCIAL STYLE Model

Since the research on SOCIAL STYLE was initially completed in the early 1960s, companies around the globe have used it to develop sales professionals, leaders, managers, and teams. Millions of users in over 100 countries have benefited from learning their SOCIAL STYLE and how to use Versatility to apply it to increase their success. A comment in the early years frequently heard from attendees was: "This is interesting, but what do we use it for?"

That was a great point, and TRACOM started working on applications that would help learners apply SOCIAL STYLEs in all parts of their lives. One of the first things that related to selling was how the Needs of each SOCIAL STYLE could be applied to Messaging. When applied, it was apparent that it worked very well. The next application focused on how meetings could be organized by Style and again the outcomes showed that this paid off with more wins and better relationships. This next section shows how the Style concept can be pragmatically applied to these two areas plus several others shown below:

- Developing key messages and compelling statements

- Evoking the right feelings

- Organizing meetings

- Negotiating

- Anticipating questions

SOCIAL STYLE will also be applied in the remaining sections of the book such as Solution Selling, Baggage Handling, Decision Mapping, Presentations, and Win-Loss Reviews. Applying Styles in these areas gains improved results in connecting with others. And that is the beginning of positive relationships, trust, and higher win rates.

Key Messages by SOCIAL STYLE

Often, in preparation for meetings, sales people ask: "What are my key messages?" Frequently, they end up creating messages that they themselves would like to hear. In other words, they sell to themselves. However, their audience may be different!

To make this simple, start by assuming that there is only one person with whom you are meeting. You are probably thinking, "But what if there are multiple styles in the audience?" This is reasonable, and you will learn about how to handle this situation in the chapter on Decision Mapping. The following charts give some examples of how you can tailor messages to each SOCIAL STYLE.

ANALYTICAL

- *Here's what we have done so far...*
- *We have looked at this data...*
- *From this, we understand...*
- *We are making these assumptions...*
- *These are the risks we see....*
- *Based on this, we recommend....*

DRIVING

- *We will produce the results you are looking for*
- *Our team will produce quick wins*
- *We have an "A" team with "X" years of experience*
- *We have done this before*
- *We can start immediately*
- *You need to put your best people on the project*

AMIABLE

- *Here's what will stay the same and what will change*
- *We have done this many times before*
- *You may call the following references*
- *We pledge to work collaboratively*
- *Change management is the most important thing*

EXPRESSIVE

- *We are very excited about helping you with implementing your vision*
- *You will be the global leader when this is completed*
- *This will be a major leap forward for you and your organization*
- *Our senior executives are completely behind this*

Meeting Behaviors by SOCIAL STYLE

This chart will help you understand that types of behavior you are likely to encounter when meeting with each Style.

ANALYTICAL

The Analytical Style will typically be less social and perhaps even awkward at the beginning of a meeting. Their posture may be rigid and likely will not have strong eye contact. Analytical people generally like to listen to the issues being presented and don't participate until the discussion is well underway, and, at that point, they may start asking considered questions.

DRIVING

The Driving Style will likely be less social and show an eagerness to get down to business. They can have strong eye contact and ask challenging questions and state their position directly. They are frequently impatient. If slightly bored, the Driving Style will try to take control or disengage and break out their smart phone.

AMIABLE

The Amiable Style will show noticeable warmth throughout the meeting. They may nod their heads in encouragement. They will be easy to socialize with at the beginning of the meeting. Amiable people may not ask any questions at all. And since they avoid disagreements, it may be necessary to encourage them to share their thoughts and concerns and make it safe for them to do so.

EXPRESSIVE

Expressive Style people will be friendly and approachable at the beginning of a meeting. They likely will talk more than anyone during the meeting and will bounce around from subject to subject. They are likely to offer opinions about many things. Finally, they may mix in humor or non-topic related items, even when not appropriate.

SOCIAL STYLE and Feelings

The second application of SOCIAL STYLEs deals with the "messy" side of interactions. This section will show why this book is titled *Adaptive Selling*.

Normally, individuals or teams prepare for meetings by focusing on what they are going to discuss or present: factual things, getting the deck ready, making sure that their work-plans and estimates are correct. This is preparation on the "hard side" of selling.

At a major account where the team was preparing for a final pitch to a large potential client, a team member posed the question: "How do we want the audience to feel after our session?" What a great line of thought it turned out to be. The discussion that followed demonstrated how to apply Style to determine how to help the client feel positive about the meeting. So, what feelings would you want each SOCIAL STYLE to have and express after a successful meeting?

This application combines **two of the themes** of this book— Understanding how SOCIAL STYLE and Versatility can help you connect and build better relationships plus Preparation with an emphasis on the "soft side" of selling. Let's explore what each Style may express as the result of adding a focus on their feelings when planning the meeting.

Analytical Styles frequently express their satisfaction with a meeting through phrases such as:

- "They were well organized with a logical agenda."

- "They are working hard to understand us."

- "They aren't pushy or salesy."

- "They knew the facts and had good processes and tools."

- "I liked it when they showed us all of their data and assumptions and even offered to provide more."

- "It was good they said they couldn't answer some of our questions without further research, and that they will get back to us later with responses."

- "They were aware of the risks and had plans to mitigate."

When a salesperson has a bad meeting, the Analytical Style client will say things such as: "It was a complete sales pitch," or, "They tried to sell us what they thought we wanted versus what we want." Or worse yet, "They weren't prepared and had no evidence of how their proposal would ensure a successful outcome."

The **Driving Style** client might express their feelings about a good meeting by saying things such as:

- "They had a good agenda and got right to the main points."

- "They didn't waste my time."

- "I like that they are confident they can produce the results we want on time and on budget."

- "It's great that they can produce quick wins."

- "Their accelerators will save us time and money."

- "They answered my tough questions."

- "They challenged me and they were right."

- "Their folks are very experienced and have done this before."

If a salesperson has a bad meeting, the Driving Style client will say things such as: "It was a complete waste of time!" or, "They will take forever to get this done." Or worse yet, "They spent all their time on chit-chat and didn't focus on our business."

The Expressive Style customer shows their satisfaction with a meeting through phrases such as:

- "They really are excited about working with us."

- "They appreciate and admire our vision and what we want to achieve."

- "They say we will be the best in the business after we do this."

- "Their CEO, who came to the meeting, was very supportive of this project."

- "They will be fun to work with!"

- "They understand me."

When the Expressive Style client experiences a bad meeting, they will say things such as: "They put out so many details that they lost track of what I want to happen!" or, "They will take forever to get this done." Or worse yet, "They had no creativity or excitement in their proposal; it's just a bunch of meaningless garbage."

Following a good meeting, we hope for **Amiable Style participants** to say things such as:

- "I really like them."

- "They will fit in with our people and culture."

- "They fully understand the business and the people and issues involved."

- "It's great that they have done this many times before."

• "Their team really seems to work well together in addressing our issues."

• "They won't leave us hanging out to dry! They back their solutions and will personally help us succeed."

Amiable Style clients who experience a bad meeting will say things such as: "They only care about getting our order," or "They told us nothing about who they are and why we should trust them with our business." Or worst of all, "They care nothing about how their solution will impact our people!"

The evocation of these positive feelings from each Style indicates a successful meeting. We have connected to the individuals. If the meeting was a final presentation during a sales effort, then your chances of winning would be very high.

So take the time to use SOCIAL STYLEs to avoid negative feelings. They can be impossible to overcome, especially ones with underlying statements such as:

Analytical Style: "They didn't understand what we wanted. Instead, they tried to sell us on what they thought we needed. Also, they were high pressure and too salesy."

Driving Style: "I simply didn't have confidence that they could produce the results I wanted. They seemed plodding and slow. They couldn't answer my questions very well and didn't have relevant experience."

Expressive Style: "They didn't seem excited about working with us! They also wanted to do their vision and not mine."

Amiable Style: "I just didn't like them. They aren't people-oriented and are pushy."

Organizing Meetings by Style

One of the most valuable applications of the SOCIAL STYLE Model is the organization of meetings according to behavioral style. Below are the potential building blocks for a presentation or meeting. Write these or others that you find relevant by Style position on Post-It pads using different colors for each Style. When preparing for a sales meeting with clients, arrange these by the Styles you need to win over. Do this on a wall or flip chart with input from others you are working with to win the sale.

Meetings with the Driving Style

Attempt to socialize briefly at the beginning, but be ready to get down to business quickly. Don't be put off when this Style quickly thumbs through your presentation or materials. If they do this, then it confirms that we are likely dealing with the Driving Style.

Other key Driving Style Tips:

• Start with an agenda.

• Put a summary of the main points on the first page. The summary should be focused on what results will be delivered and when. Consider having a placemat that is a one-page version of the summary in front of each participant in formal group meetings.

• Emphasize quick wins and show key dates

• Tell them what you want from them. Be sure to emphasize that you need their best people just as you are providing yours. Show how and when you want them involved.

• Have the project organization chart ready.

• Have a section on the experience and biographies of your key players.

• Show references and credentials emphasizing similar projects and the results produced. Put supporting details onto the back of the presentation. The following are *the most important* building blocks for the Driving Style. This is the suggested order:

Meetings with the Expressive Style

• Expressive Style clients will want to start with socializing.

• Start by showing your understanding of *their* vision.
Embrace it! Tell them how excited you are about it. Ask them
if you have it right. Remember, they like to participate early.

• Have one of your senior executives present if possible and
have them introduce themselves at the beginning.

• If your senior executives cannot be present, then have them
on a call or a video.

• If that isn't possible, then have a highly personalized letter
from them at the very beginning of the session.

• Show them what success will look like—for example,

leapfrogging competitors.

• Show them how a successful outcome will enhance their reputation for innovation, etc.

• The presentation should be detail-light, but have an appendix that you can show them if they ask. However, it is doubtful that they will.

• Make the presentation as graphical as possible. Consider using other visuals such as professionally prepared charts, demos, animations, or videos.

• Make sure to highlight their personal involvement in the "Project Organization" and "How We Will Work Together" sections.

Meetings with the Amiable Style

Remember these are the "people people." They want to have an opportunity to know those who work with them on a personal basis. They want to be certain that others who are important to them are on board with any decision. Take time to socialize at the beginning of meetings with clients with an Amiable Style. Don't be in a rush to get down to business. If you do, you may come across as uncaring and impersonal—both very negative outcomes for someone with an Amiable Style.

When it is time to get down to business:

• Start with a section on "Our Understanding of Your Situation." Ask for their thoughts on how well it aligns with yours.

• Show previous similar projects that have been successful in order to reassure them.

• Discuss the change-management risks and how you will mitigate them, especially related to people who are impacted.

• Mention the tools and processes you have that will mitigate risks.

• Emphasize the experience of your people.

• Show how you will work together in a collaborative way.

Meetings with the Analytical Style

Limit socializing at the beginning as these people will want to get into the agenda and the purpose of the meeting. Trying to be too personal with an Analytical Style can work against you as these people don't like disclosing too much about themselves personally.

• Present them with an agenda, preferably prior to the actual meeting.

• Start with "Your Understanding of Their Situation." Review with them what has been done, the problems and risks that were uncovered, and the assumptions that are being made. Have a tone of humbleness when you present this. You don't understand everything and they know it. Ask them for any changes or additions that may have missed.

• Don't pressure them with leading questions.

• The Analytical Style can be very skeptical of credentials. Show why and how they are relevant. Show lessons learned. For example, admitting mistakes by saying how that helped change what you would do differently in the future and for their project.

• When you demonstrate your tools, processes, and methods, show how they are designed to reduce risk. Don't describe these as accelerators, which could raise concerns for them.

• Provide details around your solution and how you arrived at it.

• Don't expect a quick decision; allow them time to reflect and review.

Negotiating with the Different SOCIAL STYLEs

The SOCIAL STYLE Model can be very helpful in negotiations. Remember that each Style has its own needs and these help you determine how to approach them, how to use time with them, and how they make decisions.

Negotiating with Analytical and the Driving Style Clients

CONTROLS EMOTIONS

ANALYTICAL
NEED: TO BE RIGHT

The first thing to know is that the Analytical Style will pay more. There are two principal reasons for this: first, they will pay more for what they see is a lower risk proposition. Second, they will pay more for a solution that is based on a thorough understanding of their needs.

In dealing with Analytical Styles, remember not to pressure them. Give them time and space.

They want transparency. Show them everything: assumptions, work plans, timelines and so on.

Lastly, they don't like to negotiate and go back and forth on price. So, start with close to your best price.

DRIVING
NEED: RESULTS

The Driving Style likes to negotiate, so never start with your best price. But remember fast actions that get results are more important to this Style than the lowest price.

This Style also like gain/pain sharing contracts because they believe that this type arrangement gives them more control.

Quick wins are also attractive to this style. We may win because not only can we produce desired results, but we can do so more quickly.

Finally, challenge The Driving Style by such things as demanding their best people for the project.

ASKS ⟵——————————————⟶ TELLS

DISPLAYS EMOTIONS

Negotiating with Amiable and the Expressive Style Clients

CONTROLS EMOTIONS

ASKS ← → TELLS

AMIABLE
NEED: PERSONAL SECURITY

The Amiable Style wants reassurance, so heavily reference relevant credentials

Make sure that you are offering standard terms and conditions that have used by many other organizations

Reassure further by showing what you are doing to mitigate the people risks

Don't pressure them

Engage colleagues who they respect both internal and external to their organization

Show the project contingencies

EXPRESSIVE
NEED: PERSONAL APPROVAL

Like the Analytical Style, Expressive Styles will pay more. Why, because we can help them achieve their vision and make them look good.

Show how our enablement of their vision will make them industry leading.

Also, give recognition opportunities...offer that they appear and speak at marketing events and also welcome potential client visits.

The Expressive Style may be open to connecting their decision to such items as achieving the best metrics in their industry or being recognized as a leader in their industry or field.

DISPLAYS EMOTIONS

A Look at Negotiating with Each SOCIAL STYLE In-depth

Tensions often arise when a sales conversation enters the negotiation phase. Both you and your customer have something to lose if the negotiation breaks down or if one side agrees to terms and conditions they later regret. Similarly, the give-and-take of a sales negotiation can also be a positive experience resulting in a mutually satisfactory agreement.

A sales negotiation typically begins after the customer has indicated they are interested in buying from you if you can work out satisfactory terms and conditions. How you open the negotiating session sets the tone for the entire negotiation process. The following advice will help you prepare to conduct contractual negotiations productively with each of the four SOCIAL STYLEs.

Driving Style

When negotiating, your Driving Style customers will be very direct in their behavior. Since negotiations tend to be the part of the sales conversation where there is the greatest tension, they may move toward their Backup Behavior and take control of situations. Backup Behavior occurs under stress and is an extreme form of a Style's basic behaviors. It is an attempt by the Style to reduce their tension. It is never productive to a task or relationship. Be particularly aware of this type of behavior and watch for signs these customers are feeling a higher-than-normal level of stress, such as raising their voices and becoming more animated than usual.

These customers will usually be forthright and negotiate with you in a direct, business-like manner. They might be verbally confrontational as they push for achieving terms and conditions they have set as goals. These customers are likely to dominate the negotiation session, at least until they have made their objectives clear and are assured you will help them achieve those objectives. They like to be in control and may try to take control of the negotiation session, especially if they feel an alternative to negotiating with you is simply to walk away.

Plan to interact with this customer in a direct, businesslike manner. Remember, people with this SOCIAL STYLE are naturally competitive, so be sure to position yourself as being on their team to help them achieve their goals, not as an adversary in the negotiation process. Prepare to negotiate in a clear and logical way, without distraction. Be prepared to give these customers options so they can feel they are in charge by being the one who decides. Identify in advance where you have flexibility and can offer this customer options and alternatives to such things as timelines, nature of the product or service, or pricing and payment terms. Also, be prepared with facts and proofs that support the need for the terms and conditions you propose. This can be especially important for these customers since they may challenge your position or assumptions.

Driving Style customers will not hesitate to express their opinions about the terms and conditions you propose. They may dominate the negotiation session for a while before allowing you an opportunity to speak again. They may try to take charge of the negotiation session by telling you exactly what must be included in the agreement. This is a way for them to maintain control. By nature, these individuals control their emotions, so unless they are feeling shock or anger about your proposal they will likely appear neutral throughout a typical negotiation process.

Once you reach an agreement on terms and conditions, they will want to move quickly in concluding the negotiation and the sales process instead of exploring the pros and cons of other options. They prefer to make decisions for themselves, but you should collaborate with them to develop an action plan for delivering on the agreed-upon products or services. If these customers do not like any of the terms and conditions you are offering, you will not have to guess what they think or how they feel. They will tell you. In such situations, be prepared to explain how your proposed terms and conditions will better enable them to achieve their stated objectives. If they strongly disagree with your position or are resistant to what you are saying, they may become outwardly defensive. They will be verbally forceful and will try to assert some sort of control or influence, possibly challenging your information. Though they don't usually show a lot of facial animation, their expressions will often show their frustration. These individuals will not hesitate to express their opinions. They may dominate the conversation for a while before allowing you an opportunity to speak again. They might try to take charge of the situation by telling you what needs to be done. This is also a way for them to maintain control.

Be aware that these individuals enjoy debate. Be direct in bringing up potentially uncomfortable parts of the sales negotiation (such as price), but be careful not to let the discussion turn into a contest they will be motivated to win. These customers can even appear forceful when making their points; however, unless they are obviously frustrated or insistent that you give in to non-negotiable terms, accept this behavior as simply being a part of their SOCIAL STYLE. If negotiation sessions become particularly intense, these customers can be kept in a more productive state if you show that you understand their point of view, and you communicate with them on a logical basis. Show them how you can help them achieve the results they need. Driving Style individuals are responsive to facts, so if they focus on extraneous issues, bring the negotiation discussion back to the hard data. Reinforce that negotiating terms and conditions is intended to be a means of ensuring that the ultimate purpose of the negotiation is fulfilled.

Expressive Style

When negotiating, expect Expressive Style people to be animated and to share their opinions freely. As tension increases during negotiations, they may move toward their Backup Behavior, which is to attack. These customers will be very direct when negotiating and will at times say things without pausing to consider the implications or your point of view. They may respond defensively if you question or disagree with their counterproposal. Remember, they may have difficulty separating disagreements about their ideas from rejection of them as individuals. If your customer has an emotional reaction to an element of your offer, they may interrupt you before you have a chance to fully present your offer. They might dominate discussion until they are satisfied they have fully communicated their opinions about your offer. If these customers feel highly stressed during the negotiation, they may display hostility toward you and confront you personally rather than focus on reaching a mutually satisfactory agreement. From the beginning of the negotiation to the end, be warm and communicative with these customers. Even when you are engaged in an intense negotiation, interact with them in a supportive way that shows you fully support their aspirations, either business objectives or their personal goals. Let them know the purpose of the negotiation is to reach a mutually satisfactory agreement that helps them fulfill those aspirations. Remember, people with this SOCIAL STYLE are naturally competitive, so be sure to position yourself as a teammate, and not as an adversary in the negotiation process.

These individuals will show you how they feel. If they are not defensive about the give-and-take of negotiation, they may react positively to the possibility of the negotiation leading to positive outcomes. Keep in mind that these customers like to be involved, so instead of telling them the terms you would like to include, collaborate with them to identify terms and conditions that will satisfy both of you. This will appeal to their need for recognition and involvement. Even though negotiations can become intense, feel free to use humor to diffuse tension. These customers are oriented toward spontaneity and like to have fun, even in business settings. Humor can help in many situations and is particularly effective with these individuals.

If you do not agree to their terms, choose your words carefully in letting them know. Expressive Style people do not readily distinguish a rejection of their ideas from a personal rejection of them. In such cases they may revert to their Backup Behavior, which is to attack. Consequently, their response may be blunt and personal. They might bring up issues that are tangential to the discussion and can come across as irrational. If this occurs, allow them to play out their emotional reaction before returning to a previous point in the conversation where you were in agreement. Be prepared for the possibility that this customer may have an emotional response to the specific terms or conditions of your offer. Of course, this does not mean that you should avoid having the discussion, but anticipate possible reactions this customer might have. Help these customers separate their emotions about a negotiation topic from the objective facts. Summarize or restate their opinions in a calm and straightforward way to let them know you understand their concerns and then explain your rationale for your own position.

Because these individuals have the capacity to react in a very emotional way, it is easy to lose control of conversations. If this is happening, listen to what they are saying without responding defensively. Accept the reality of the emotions they are expressing without getting personally involved in it. Do not appear to counter-attack or the situation may rapidly spiral out of control. Once they have adequately expressed their emotions, redirect them to the issues at hand. Remember that Expressive Style people often calm down quickly after they've vented their emotions, so it's possible they will soon be able to discuss the issue more rationally.

Be sure to keep these people involved. When negotiating with them, be sure to ask for their feedback, opinions, and ideas. This is not difficult since they do not hesitate to express themselves. Approach the negotiation as an open and free exchange, where the customer is providing as much input about the potential terms of the agreement as you are. When these customers tell you they need to include a term or condition you find acceptable, be positive and acknowledge their contribution to the process.

Amiable Style

Unlike Driving or Analytical Style customers, these customers are not interested in hearing about a variety of options or examining them in detail. Put forth the best set of terms and conditions you feel this customer will accept, but keep these individuals actively engaged in the negotiation conversation and process. To do this, confirm their agreement at each step of the process by asking if they have any questions or concerns. This is important because you may need to bring to the surface issues you think might be important to them but they may be hesitant to bring up themselves. Asking about questions or concerns provides them with an entry into the conversation and reassures them they can have a positive effect on the outcome of the negotiation session.

With these customers, it is often helpful to begin by talking about terms and conditions upon which you are confident you have their full agreement. This may help put the customer at ease before you move on to discussing issues where there might be less alignment of views. While they normally enjoy talking with others, these customers may become less talkative during negotiation and might not fully share their true opinions. They often display their discomfort nonverbally through their facial expressions, minimal use of hand gestures, and "leaning back" body posture. Trust is very important for these customers. If they have a good relationship with you, they will be more likely to accept and respond in a positive way to your negotiating points. When presenting the terms and conditions you would like to include in the final agreement, be sure they are aware you are striving to help them achieve a mutually satisfactory agreement.

Amiable Style people display their emotions, therefore their feelings about your message will probably be apparent either through what they say or their nonverbal responses. If they are not surprised by your message, they will openly express how they feel about the matter and the conversation will usually be two-sided and collaborative. If they are shocked or disagree with your message, it will be obvious they are unhappy, though they may be less forthcoming than others might be. They may remain relatively quiet and withhold their opinions. Their Backup Behavior is to acquiesce, so they might tacitly agree with what you are saying and privately disagree. If they feel very strongly about your message, they are likely to respond in an emotional way and may share some of their opinions and feelings.

These individuals are not usually highly vocal or abrasive, but they can be abrupt when upset. They may try to end the conversation quickly without fully expressing themselves or searching for an agreeable resolution to the issue. These customers might feel uncomfortable or even threatened by a difficult negotiation process. If you believe they are not fully and openly participating, there may be some issue they are reluctant to mention. If they seem to be holding back, make it safe for them to negotiate with you. An effective way to help these individuals engage in productive negotiation is to ask open-ended questions to help them share their thoughts. Let them know that by negotiating a mutually satisfactory agreement their work situation will improve, and this might include their relationships with others. This approach can help them to overcome their natural hesitancy about initiating ideas or actions.

Since negotiations can become highly demanding, the Amiable Style customer may acquiesce or seem to agree. As a result, it may not be immediately obvious to you if these customers disagree with you during the negotiation. At times they may appear to be going along with the terms you put forth even though they may have significant unexpressed concerns. Be aware their feelings are not likely to disappear and may not surface until you attempt to close the sale. If the disagreement is significant, they will later put up obstacles to concluding the negotiation. They may even try to nullify their explicit agreements by citing factors beyond their personal control, such as a committee vetoing the deal or the needs of the organization changing. This allows them to appear to agree with your terms and conditions personally while putting the blame elsewhere. Do not end the negotiation conversation if you suspect this customer has unresolved questions or concerns. If this is the case, the impacts may linger and remain unaddressed, leading to more difficulty and making them find excuses to cause the sale to fall through later. Before concluding the negotiation, take the time to confirm that the customer is truly in agreement, and is committed to following through on negotiated terms and conditions.

Analytical Style

When negotiating, Analytical Style people might remain relatively quiet until others share their opinions before taking part in the negotiation discussion and offering their own viewpoints. They are most comfortable when they have heard different sides of the debate and information they may not have considered. In addition, they wish to avoid the risk of making the wrong decision. Consequently, they do not like to make quick decisions; they might want you to provide your input on the steps you believe necessary to reach a satisfactory agreement. If they are uneasy about any of the terms or conditions you suggest, they will likely seek ways to avoid making a decision until they can get more information and examine the issues in more depth.

Plan to approach the negotiation session in a straightforward, cooperative, business-like manner. Prepare to present your proposed terms and conditions using a clear and logical approach in such a way that demonstrates your proposal is well thought out and has merit. Be prepared to explain fully the meaning and implications of your proposed terms and conditions. Have ready specific reasons why your suggested terms and conditions are necessary. This is important for Analytical Style people since they will want a sound rationale to help them consider and accept your negotiating points.

Begin the negotiation conversation in a friendly but professional way. Analytical Style people are concerned with both process and making the right decision. State that you would like to put forward the best terms and conditions for discussion and examination that you believe will lead to a productive outcome for both of you.

When negotiating specific issues, take time to summarize the main points and discuss things in a rational way in terms of pros and cons, implications of each decision, and so on. Remember, these customers like to examine all sides of an issue before making a decision. If you do not allow time to do this, they will likely want to postpone concluding the negotiation process until they have had time to think.

These customers will not be interested in negotiating with you if they believe you are ignoring important details or facts, trying to persuade them on an overly emotional level, or pressing for immediate decisions. Avoid glossing over important details or facts, making dramatic, emotional appeals, or pressing for immediate decisions as they value rational thinking and logical approaches.

Encourage these customers to have an active dialogue with you. Listen carefully to their questions and statements, and probe to determine if there are any issues of concern to them that you have not adequately addressed. If necessary, allow meeting breaks and let them spend some time thinking about your proposed terms and conditions before following up with them.

Because these individuals control their emotions, they are unlikely to display very much emotion about the proposition. This is not to say they won't be concerned, but they may not express very much feeling around the message. If they are not surprised or shocked, they are likely to remain calm and may take some time to think about what you tell them. They won't necessarily rush into a problem-solving state of mind, but they might want you to provide your opinion about steps to be taken to address the issue. Even if they are upset, Analytical Style people will be eager to return to a rational and comfortable conversation. You can help bring the conversation back to a more productive state by approaching them in a rational way. Reiterate your reasoning and the evidence that supports your position.

When discussions involve potential points of disagreement, these customers may avoid direct eye contact with you and others more than usual (an indication of their Backup Behavior). They may show their discomfort by frequently shifting their body position in their chairs, leaning back, and holding their arms and hands close to their body. In addition, if the negotiation becomes particularly intense, these individuals may display their discomfort by becoming quieter than usual and by disengaging from the conversation. They may even try to withdraw from the negotiation conversation. However, when they feel strongly about an issue, they can be passionate negotiators.

USING SOCIAL STYLE AND VERSATILITY TO IMPROVE YOUR EMOTIONAL INTELLIGENCE AND SALES RESULTS

Versatility and Emotional Intelligence

We can't change our SOCIAL STYLE and we can't get anyone else to change theirs, but we can improve our Versatility if we so choose. What comprises Versatility? We will see that it is strongly related to emotional intelligence.

Versatility is the third dimension of the SOCIAL STYLE Model. While one's SOCIAL STYLE will not change from group to group, Versatility is much more dynamic. This is good news because it means it can be improved. Any Style can have high or low Versatility. Versatility can be increased by the following steps:

- Knowing who we are—our SOCIAL STYLE position

- Controlling our potentially inappropriate behaviors

- Knowing the SOCIAL STYLE of those we are dealing with and what their needs are as well as what elements of their Style may create higher tension for you

• Adapting (Doing Something) for their Style to generate productive energy and tension that helps them with their needs and goals while enabling us meet our goals

Daniel Goleman, the noted psychologist and writer, states that emotional intelligence is more important than both IQ and education in predicting business success.[5] This can also be true in our personal lives.

Goleman's findings can also be applied to Versatility, which can be defined as emotional intelligence enhanced by an understanding of the SOCIAL STYLE Model. Personal experience and major research studies have proven that Versatility scores correlate with business success. The higher a person's level of Versatility, the better their performance and they tend to earn significantly more than those with lower Versatility.[6] In the organizations with which we have dealt, Versatility scores tend to increase as the level of hierarchy increases. In other words, higher ranking people generally have higher Versatility.

Research by Dr. Travis Bradberry showed that 90 percent of top performers have high EQ. Your emotional intelligence (Versatility) is responsible for 58 percent of your job performance.[7] And best of all, people who have high EQ (Versatility) earn on average $29,000 more than low EQ counterparts.

BECOMING MORE VERSATILE

| KNOWING WHO YOU ARE | CONTROLLING YOURSELF AND INAPPROPRIATE BEHAVIORS | KNOWING THE OTHER PERSON'S STYLE | ADAPTING AND DOING SOMETHING FOR OTHERS |

Knowing Who You Are and How You Appear to Others

KNOWING WHO YOU ARE

| KNOWING WHO YOU ARE | CONTROLLING YOURSELF AND INAPPROPRIATE BEHAVIORS | KNOWING THE OTHER PERSON'S STYLE | ADAPTING AND DOING SOMETHING FOR OTHERS |

A key component of learning SOCIAL STYLE includes understanding what Styles do under stress. Many facilitators have participants place their name on a small sticky note in the Style quadrant where they think they belong. This sticky-note activity is usually at a break before the results from the SOCIAL STYLE and Versatility Profile Reports are distributed.

Guess what always happens? A minimum of 50 percent— sometimes as high as 75 percent—consider themselves as belonging to a SOCIAL STYLE different from the quadrant where others see them behaving. This seems to be true no matter the company or organization where SOCIAL STYLE training has been implemented. This reflects the fact that most people are not self-aware of their typical behaviors. It is a common cognitive bias known as the *Self-Perception Bias.*

Another thing to understand is that everyone can use behavior from each Style for short periods of time. You may be an Expressive Style, but sometimes you might use behaviors of an Amiable Style. At other times, you may show some behaviors of an Analytical or Driving Style. Another way to describe this is to think of your Style as your home base. However you may have a front porch on your Style that has room for you to use behaviors from the other three quadrants for short periods of time. Remember, your SOCIAL

STYLE is the behaviors others observe you using most frequently. As a result, this is how they expect us to behave, and it influences how they interact with us. In fact, others may see behaviors we might display that are not from our typical Style position as confusing and short-term.

The Possible Inappropriate Behaviors of SOCIAL STYLEs

CONTROLLING YOURSELF

| KNOWING WHO YOU ARE | CONTROLLING YOURSELF AND INAPPROPRIATE BEHAVIORS | KNOWING THE OTHER PERSON'S STYLE | ADAPTING AND DOING SOMETHING FOR OTHERS |

Let's look more deeply at each Style in this context starting with the Expressive Style:

- Expressive Styles can talk too much.

- This frequently comes across as not listening to others.

- When stressed, Expressive Styles can attack personally. Often, they regret this later.

- They can also express opinions about everything, even when not asked.

- Expressive Styles sometimes tell too many stories that are not always appropriate to the situation. The Driving and Analytical Styles normally find Expressive Style stories unrelated to the topic at hand.

• Expressive Style people can sometimes offend others by countering stories with other stories. An individual may tell a story. An out-of-control Expressive Style may then counter with what they think is an even better story. This Expressive Style person likely didn't acknowledge the other person's story. This behavior can cause disconnects in the relationship.

• Expressive Style people sometimes repeat points too often. This happens when they make a point that they think is important and no one acknowledges them. So, they repeat it again. Then, maybe they do it again in another way. This can be highly irritating, especially to the more Control Responsive Styles of Driving and Analytical.

• The Expressive Style is undisciplined and free-flowing in how they use time.

The Possible Inappropriate Behaviors of the Driving Style:

• When stressed, the Driving Style can come across as autocratic and people-insensitive.

• The Driving Style can sometimes seem to be antisocial, judgmental, and off-putting.

• This Style can be too impatient with others, which can hurt harmony and be seen as rude.

• The Driving Style can come across as hoarding information in order to gain power or control.

• The Driving Style often interrupts others when they think they understand the issue or have made a quick decision and want to move on to something else. They don't see this behavior as being rude whereas others may be offended and feel discounted.

• The Driving Style can come across as not caring about what others think or not being open to other approaches.

• They can be over-challenging with questions that aren't helpful.

• The Driving Style can be over-controlling both in meetings and socially.

• The Driving Style is not good at listening.

• The Driving Style is disciplined in how they use time….so be efficient with them!

The Possible Inappropriate Behaviors of the Analytical Style:

• Similar to the Driving Style, the Analytical Style can come across as unsocial, secretive, and unengaged.

• When stressed, Analytical Style people may retreat to their "data cave" where they don't like to be bothered. This behavior is frustrating to those on the right half of the quadrant system, such as the Expressive and Driving Styles.

• Analytical Style people can be seen as indecisive for taking too long to make decisions.

• They often appear too unwilling to take risks.

• The Analytical Style can come across as a barrier to progress.

• They can be seen as cautious or guarded communicators holding back information from others.

• They are disciplined in how they use time and prefer to focus on a specific issue rather than multi-tasking.

The Possible Inappropriate Behaviors of the Amiable Style:

• When stressed, the Amiable Style will tend go along with what others want, even though they know better.

• The Amiable Style is hesitant to initiate things, especially conflict or disagreement.

• They seek to maintain harmony when candor may be needed.

• As a result of stress, Amiable Style people can fail to take necessary actions or to reveal contrary information or opinions.

• They don't want confrontation even when it is necessary.

• Like the Analytical Style, they can take too long to make decisions.

• They are reluctant to take risks.

• The Amiable Style can also be seen as over-socializing and too personal with little concern for the business issues.

• The Amiable Style is unstructured in how they use time.

ADAPTING TO THE OTHER PERSON'S SOCIAL STYLE

| KNOWING WHO YOU ARE | CONTROLLING YOURSELF AND INAPPROPRIATE BEHAVIORS | KNOWING THE OTHER PERSON'S STYLE | ADAPTING AND DOING SOMETHING FOR OTHERS |

Previously, we covered how to determine another person's SOCIAL STYLE with the observation test. A better alternative is to use TRACOM's multi-rater assessment or the SOCIAL STYLE Navigator application.

We also covered what the needs are of the different SOCIAL STYLEs.

SOCIAL STYLE NEED

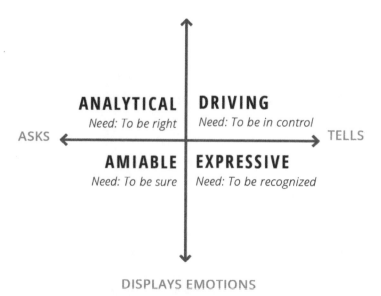

CONTROLS EMOTIONS

ANALYTICAL | DRIVING
Need: To be right | *Need: To be in control*

ASKS ← → TELLS

AMIABLE | EXPRESSIVE
Need: To be sure | *Need: To be recognized*

DISPLAYS EMOTIONS

DOING SOMETHING FOR OTHERS

KNOWING WHO YOU ARE	CONTROLLING YOURSELF AND INAPPROPRIATE BEHAVIORS	KNOWING THE OTHER PERSON'S STYLE	ADAPTING AND DOING SOMETHING FOR OTHERS

The next step is to adapt to the individual Styles of others and do something to help them with their goals.

This is critical to improving your relationships, earning trust, and increasing your sales performance. It doesn't mean that you need to change who you are and your SOCIAL STYLE. It means that you need to learn a few new ways of using your Style when working with those whose Style is different. Keep in mind that adapting is hardest for those who find themselves in diagonal quadrants. For example, it can be challenging for Expressive and Analytical Styles to deal with each other, and the same is true for the Driving Style dealing with Amiable Style colleagues or clients. Opposites are simply different in many fundamental ways.

Adapting doesn't mean becoming a chameleon. Instead, it means respecting how others like to be communicated with and what they value. Adapting also means knowing what not to do with them, and what they can do that might create higher tension for you.

There are common techniques, no matter what Style we are, to treat each of the other Styles. For example, with the Driving and Analytical Styles, be prepared to get down to business and have an agenda. With Analytical and Amiable Styles, don't pressure them for a decision. Let's look at some key ways you can increase your Versatility and effectiveness with each Style.

HOW AN ANALYTICAL STYLE CAN ADAPT TO
AND HELP THE OTHER STYLES

CONTROLS EMOTIONS

ANALYTICALS

DRIVING
· Speed up
· Get to the point
· Be prepared to answer
  their questions
· Show confidence that
  results can be achieved
· Answer questions directly

ASKS ←   → TELLS

AMIABLES
· Socialize
· Don't worry as much about
  structure and going off-point
· Tell them who you have
  talked with
· Reassure them that we have
  done this many times before

EXPRESSIVES
· Socialize
· Speed up
· Don't worry as much about
  structure and going off-point
· Ask them for their advice
  and coaching
· Seek their advice
· Flatter them

DISPLAYS EMOTIONS

HOW AN EXPRESSIVE STYLE CAN ADAPT TO
AND HELP THE OTHER STYLES

CONTROLS EMOTIONS

ANALYTICALS
- Don't spend too much time socializing
- Have an agenda
- Bring as much detail as you can
- Be transparent
- Tell them what you have done but be factual
- Don't pressure or expect immediate decisions
- Ask and probe

DRIVING
- Get down to business quickly
- Have an agenda
- Be fact based
- Anticipate and prepare for their questions
- Show confidence that results can be achieved
- Answer questions directly
- Tell them what you want from them
- Keep emotions under control

ASKS ← ———————————————— → TELLS

AMIABLES
- Socialize
- Don't worry about structure and agendas
- Tell them who you have seen and what you have heard
- Reassure them that you have done this before
- Don't pressure or expect immediate decisions

EXPRESSIVES

DISPLAYS EMOTIONS

HOW AN AMIABLE STYLE CAN ADAPT TO
AND HELP THE OTHER STYLES

CONTROLS EMOTIONS

ANALYTICALS
- Don't count on extensive socializing
- Have an agenda
- Be fact based
- Don't let their limited sharing of personal information or feelings make you uncomfortable
- Bring as much detail as you have
- Ask and probe

DRIVING
- Get down to business quickly
- Have an agenda
- Be fact based
- Anticipate and prepare for their questions
- Show confidence that results can be achieved
- Answer questions directly
- Tell them what you want from them
- Keep emotions under control

ASKS ← → TELLS

EXPRESSIVES
- Socialize
- Speed up
- Don't worry as much about structure and going off-point
- Ask them for their advice and coaching
- Seek their advice
- Flatter them

AMIABLES

DISPLAYS EMOTIONS

HOW A DRIVING STYLE CAN ADAPT TO
AND HELP THE OTHER STYLES

CONTROLS EMOTIONS

ANALYTICALS
- *Don't pressure them*
- *Bring as much detail as you have*
- *Be transparent*
- *Talk with them about process*
- *Ask them about the risks they see*
- *Don't expect immediate decisions*
- *Be patient*
- *Don't pressure them*

DRIVING

ASKS ←   → TELLS

AMIABLES
- *Socialize*
- *Share something about yourself*
- *Tell them who you have talked with*
- *Don't pressure*
- *Talk with them about people issues*
- *Reassure them that you have done this before*
- *Don't expect immediate commitment*

EXPRESSIVES
- *Socialize*
- *Don't worry about structure and agendas*
- *Don't bore them with too much detail*
- *Ask about their vision*
- *Flatter them*
- *Ask for their opinions*
- *Solicit their advice and coaching*
- *Don't stare at them*
- *Don't ask them too many challenging questions*

DISPLAYS EMOTIONS

Measuring Versatility

While knowing one's SOCIAL STYLE is important, understanding the impact one's Style has on others is critical. This is measured through the third dimension of the TRACOM SOCIAL STYLE Assessment, Versatility. Versatility measures three key areas with a series of questions answered by designated raters. These dimensions are:

- Presentation

- Competence

- Feedback: some refer to this as "People Skills"

The TRACOM Profile Report shows how others rate your Versatility. While there is **no one best** SOCIAL STYLE position, Versatility does measure the impact one is having based on how they behave with others from a low to high score. People who score higher on this dimension are more successful in sales, management, and teams than those who score lower.

Equally important is the fact that almost everyone in the workplace has a modest amount of Versatility. This means lower scoring people have the capacity to be more versatile, but lack consistency in doing so. So, to gain the benefits of higher Versatility, most of us just need to work on being more aware of using our existing skills rather than attempting to learn new ones.

The good news is that Versatility is dynamic and can be improved without changing one's Style. Let's look more closely at these four dimensions.

Presentation

This is about how well we communicate with different types and different levels of people. By different types of people, we mean different SOCIAL STYLEs. For example, when presenting to the Driving Style, we may need to organize our meeting to their liking by summarizing at the very beginning, while with other Styles we may need a different approach. It also measures the appropriateness of our language for the level of the audience; in other words, do we make it easier for others to understand us?

Relevant questions include:

- Is this presentation organized so that the audience will like it?

- Does the presentation use the preferred media of the audience? Not all audiences want PowerPoint, for example.

- How well did you anticipate and answer questions? Were the examples and words you used appropriate for the audience?

Competence

Competence is the most important factor as measured by the TRACOM instrument. Competence doesn't mean technical or skills competence. It has nothing to do with IQ or education. Instead, it means how well others perceive us in achieving our goals and the extent to which we help others—especially in meeting their goals.

Important factors comprising Competence are:

• **Conscientiousness:** How reliable and dependable are we? Can we be counted on to get the job done? Dependability is the most important of the competence factors. Are you responsive? How well do you get back to people who have messaged you or to whom you made a commitment?

• **Perseverance (Resiliency or Grit):** This is a cousin of Conscientiousness and Dependability. It measures how well you keep going in spite of adversity. Do you give up too quickly, for example? When difficult or challenging situations arise, do you become frustrated and find it difficult to persist? Getting frustrated and sometimes feeling worn down might be a natural immediate reaction. However, in the long-term, this behavior can undermine others' perceptions of your Competence. If challenging circumstances or shifting priorities consistently discourage you, others may come to feel that they cannot rely on you. Work to overcome those cognitive biases that drive how you deal with adversity. These biases can be overcome through awareness and learning to see the other side of the coin.

• **Flexibility:** How well do you flex when conditions change? How open are you to other ideas? When situations change, do you adjust? If there's one thing that seems to be consistent in the modern workplace, it's change. Altering a course of action to adjust for new priorities is important. In addition, your general flexibility in helping co-workers impacts their perceptions of you. Rigid individuals are generally not seen as having high Competence.

• The Driving and Analytical Styles in particular can have a problem with being flexible. They become hell-bent on producing results or being right. The Driving Style may give quick "no way" responses to requests for changes or enhancements because they don't want to miss deadlines. Instead, they need to listen with more patience and, even if the answer is no, suggest an alternative. The Analytical Style may become rigid and inflexible until they have time to fully understand the change and its risks so they can determine if it is right for them. This can lead to missed opportunities and frustration for other more assertive Styles.

• **Optimism:** Do we see the glass as half-full or half-empty? Do we display confidence? Optimism is a dominant characteristic of CEOs and individuals with higher Versatility. Do you come across to your co-workers as unenthusiastic? While you don't have to be constantly upbeat and lively, an optimistic attitude can be important. Optimism conveys to others that difficult tasks can be accomplished successfully. Maintaining positive energy and demonstrating your confidence in the likelihood of positive outcomes can help to increase the respect and support you receive from others. And recent research has shown a side benefit of optimism: optimistic people live longer!

• **Innovation:** Are you innovative? Do you welcome innovative ideas? Not everyone is innovative, but they can welcome the good ideas of others. Innovative people, especially the Expressive Style, can block out other ideas they see as competing with their own. They must challenge themselves to grow their Versatility by considering other ideas that could be better. Ask yourself: Are you open to new ideas and to offering ideas of your own? Your ability to develop original ideas and being open to different methods of accomplishing objectives can be critical in the workplace. Your flexibility and motivation for solving problems can affect others' perceptions of your Competence. To be most effective in this area, make an effort to take an active role in generating creative ideas and in displaying openness to new methods of getting things done.

Note that the different SOCIAL STYLEs have different lenses in judging competence, especially reliability.

• The Driving Styles judge on results—particularly on time, tasks, and on budget.

• Expressive Styles judge on the innovativeness, energy, and creativity of the solution delivered.

• Analytical Styles are more about quality and durability.

• The Amiable Style focuses on user acceptance. Amiable people know, as we all should, that people risks are the biggest challenge when making major changes. They want to be sure that others who are important to them are on board.

So in summary, Competence is all about meeting our goals and helping others achieve their goals.

Feedback (People Skills)

When Dr. Merrill and Roger Reid discovered the components of Versatility through empirical research, they saw that one of the most critical dimensions was "Feedback." People with high people skills interact better with others. They accomplish more and they are valued at a high level by co-workers, customers, etc. They do so by:

• Developing and maintaining a network within their organization and with clients

• Having superior questioning, active listening, and probing skills

• Being seen as caring—showing empathy when necessary

• Creating mutually productive relationships with people of different Styles

Image

Prior to the emergence of the virtual workplace which has led to fewer and fewer in-person interactions, TRACOM's Versatility Assessment also measured Image. Image encompasses our presence, whether we dress appropriately for the situation we are in, and what people think when they first encounter us. It is especially important for first meetings. Remember mom saying, "First impressions are lasting impressions!" She was right. Most people judge others within the first ten seconds and then search for details that support their judgement. In sales, these judgements can be real barriers if they are negative about one's image. So although Image is no longer measured by TRACOM it is still an area one needs to be aware of and take steps to make certain that the way they present themselves to others is appropriate for the situation, especially in sales.

We recently met an attorney for the first time. She looked and acted like a senior lawyer who could be trusted. She had a presence, based on dress and decorum. She also questioned and listened well, and exuded confidence which reflected her Feedback skills.

Networking

Networkers develop and nurture great relationships. Relationships are important within your organization and with existing clients, including former clients and potential new ones. Networking doesn't just mean talking about the weather or sports around the coffee machine.

New employees should take to heart the need to develop a network of peers, subordinates, and mentors. This network can provide coaching and informal feedback regarding performance and career paths. Overtime, they serve as a person's personal board of directors that helps ensure their career success.

Networking by walking around can be powerful. A general manager at a friend's golf club excelled at this. He was everywhere and seemed to know everyone personally. He made time for others as a regular part of his job. Similarly, at a resort in Costa Rica, the general manager meets arriving guests at the front door when they arrive on the hotel bus from the airport.

Some have reservations about reaching out to just see how things are with others. For sure, the Driving and Analytical Styles aren't as receptive to this but Expressive and Amiable Styles likely will be, as it plays to their natural strengths. Those above-the-line folks need to practice their skills at interacting with others. The payoff is significant.

We worked for an executive who was a huge networker. He had a data file organized by cities. He would keep people's names in it and he noted each meeting or communication. He would pull up the appropriate data for a city that he would be visiting and then contact a few of his network folks to see if he could drop by or have a drink with them to catch up. His efforts frequently paid off with great opportunities. And the people in his network remembered him as someone who valued them and who in turn they valued.

Questioning, Actively Listening, and Probing

Every client who has hired us to help their sales organization shares a common need to improve in questioning, listening, and probing. One way to solve this problem is to do your homework! Think of good questions before meetings rather than counting on being able to do so on the fly. These questions should come from what you want to confirm and things that you want to know that will help move the opportunity forward.

Compare this to the traditional approach to planning meetings, which is to contemplate what a sales person wants to tell the other person.

The second problem is not listening, and that can lead to missed opportunities to probe for important information. What can happen is that people don't listen well because they are thinking of either what they are going to ask next or what they are going to say next. As a result, they may miss the nuance and emotions of what the other person is saying. For example, a person may say: "This is a real concern for us!" Instead of probing that concern just mentioned, they may ask: "What other problems do you have?" If you find yourself feeling that listening and probing is a development area for you, delve into more literature or eLearning on active listening.

A recent article by a reporter at the *New York Times* who had interviewed hundreds of CEOs concluded that one of the dominant traits that he identified among them was curiosity.[8] Great questioners and listeners possess this trait.[9]

> "...*being interested* is more important in cultivating and maintaining relationships than *being interesting*..." according to a study by Dr. Todd Kashdan, author of the book Curious."

Empathy

Professionals often lack empathic skills. In 2015, Belinda Palmer, OBE, writing in the *Harvard Business Review*,[10] shared the following quote from a British CEO of a major bank at the World Economic Forum:

> We all know it's important to be empathic, but how do I galvanize 48,000 people in my UK operations — *most of whom think that empathy is for wimps?"*

Ms. Palmer stated that most businesses still suffer from an empathy deficit. They mainly don't have this soft skill because they see empathy as non-businesslike or as a sign of weakness.

So, what is empathy? On a fundamental level, it is two things:

• Understanding the other person's feelings

• Letting them know that you understand—acknowledging

Failure comes from not acknowledging in a compassionate way. However, this acknowledgement doesn't necessarily mean that you must agree with the other person. There will be a more in-depth exploration of this in the sections on Empathy and Baggage Handling.

This concludes our introduction to SOCIAL STYLE and how useful this Model can be. Hopefully, you saw many things within the Versatility section that you can put to work, such as how you can adapt to other Styles. In addition, you can now improve your own Versatility by controlling your potentially inappropriate behaviors. If you want to really be prepared to use this powerful behavioral Model, you should seek the opportunity to get your Profile results through TRACOM's multi-rater SOCIAL STYLE Assessment process.

Additional Comments about SOCIAL STYLE and Versatility

• Our SOCIAL STYLE doesn't change beyond our teenage years. However, we can improve our Versatility if we choose to do so.

• Versatility is a choice!

• Versatility is not a good or bad scale or a measure of like or dislike. It is a measure of how much support and respect others extend to you as a result of you building a mutually productive relationship.

• The SOCIAL STYLE Model works in all cultures. In fact, the TRACOM Instrument can be applied using over 85 different sets of country norms as well as regional norms covering the globe. What many US clients have found is that it is easy for them to figure out the Style of North American and British colleagues, but it can be much more difficult when working in Asia and other non-English speaking cultures. Measuring people against the norm that represent their country leads to greater buy-in to the results and thus better outcomes. TRACOM's SOCIAL STYLE Passport allows individuals who have been profiled by TRACOM to run their data against all existing norms so one can look to see how they may be viewed in other cultures.

• Many believe that our Style is different at home with family than at work. This is not the case. If fact, in many cases, we are less Versatile at home and with friends because we feel less of a need to manage our behaviors with the people closest to us. It probably would not hurt all of us to work on our Versatility with loved ones and family.

• Many ask how SOCIAL STYLE is different from Myers Briggs and other instruments such as DiSC. There are two differences. The first is that the SOCIAL STYLE Assessment's determination of your Style is based on feedback from others, whereas the other tests utilize self-evaluation only. This is important because most of us see ourselves as behaving differently from how we are actually behaving (Self-Evaluation and Self-Perception Biases). So, the SOCIAL STYLE Profile Report gives us more accurate results and better self-awareness. The second major and critical difference is the inclusion of information on the impact one is having on others. This is the Versatility score.

SOCIAL STYLES and Loyalty

Although all Styles can be loyal, two of the Styles are more loyal than the other two. Any guesses? They are the Analytical and Amiable Styles. It takes more time to develop loyalty with Analytical Style people, but once earned, it is unwavering. Expressive Styles have the lowest loyalty. It takes a great deal of nourishment and attention to keep the loyalty of Expressive people.

Which Styles Will Pay More?

The two that will pay more are the Analytical and Expressive Styles. Why? Analytical clients will pay more if you can lower their risks. They like decisions that have less likelihood of backfiring on them. Expressive Styles will pay more if you can make them look good or be recognized for their decisions. It is all about their willingness to take risks to earn a big payoff!

Summary of How to Improve Versatility

First, we need to know and understand our normal behavior. Most of us may not know this until we receive the feedback of others.

Next, we must control our potentially inappropriate behaviors.

Third, we need to understand with whom we are dealing—determine their SOCIAL STYLE.

Finally, we should adapt to how they like to be treated and then do something to help them.

Understanding SOCIAL STYLE and Versatility can make it easier to systematically be a relationship master. This is the second major theme of this book.

ADAPTIVE SELLING IN ACTION

To start this section, let's go through a typical first meeting with a prospect.

A Meeting between EMAX and James Jacklin

Imagine that you are Alys Sanders, the global managing partner for sales and marketing for EMAX. Your firm is primarily a systems integration and outsourcing firm with 110,000 employees and $11.8 billion in revenues. Your responsibilities include the monitoring of key sales statistics produced from your CRM software. You have been asked by the firm's CEO to look into sales training.

Your firm invests 8 percent of revenue in business development. This is up from 6.2 percent two years ago. An alarming set of win/loss statistics shows your firm is winning only 28 percent of competitive bids. Formerly, your win rate had been averaging 42 percent.

Interviews with clients following a loss often show that a team has been very poor in relationship building. Teams seem to be in sales mode all the time. They also haven't taken time to understand what was really needed by the client.

Another problem that you have found is that EMAX teams have done poorly in presentations where they seemed disorganized, ill-prepared, and couldn't answer questions cogently.

A friend from another firm has referred James Jacklin to you, stating that he has a relevant background in your industry and has a training session that could be useful. You have agreed to meet with James.

James Jacklin Background:

Imagine you are James and a friend has made an introduction for you to meet Alys Sanders at EMAX. A bit of research reveals that EMAX is a large systems and integration firm with revenues of approximately $11 billion and with over 100,000 employees. You understand that Alys is responsible for sales and marketing and has an Analytical SOCIAL STYLE.

James has developed a training program that integrates the best practices and skills available and has proven that these integrated techniques work from coaching many deals. James has delivered this training to several different organizations including a large global chemical company and two very large commercial real estate companies.

To make the meeting efficient, James has put together a credentials deck that describes the training offering and client experiences.

Here's a dialogue of the meeting:

James: "Hello Alys, thanks for seeing me."

Alys: "You are welcome."

James: "I know that we only have twenty minutes, so I have put together this deck to go through, is that okay?"

Alys: "I suppose so."

James (opening the deck): "As you can see from the first page, I have worked in your industry extensively using a set of integrated tools, skills, and best practices. My training covers these areas. I have delivered this to several large organizations, including a global chemical firm and even to large commercial real estate organizations."

Alys: "What is in your training?"

James: "I'm glad you asked. As you can see on the next page, my training covers the areas shown. Are you familiar with these topics?"

Alys: "Not sure that I am."

James: "Well, SOCIAL STYLEs…" (He continues to describe the elements of Style training for the next 12 minutes.)

James: "Also, the training is highly interactive with table exercises and three role plays."

Alys: "Um."

James: "Could I come back later and spend a couple of hours going through this with you in more detail?"

Alys: "Well, I'm not sure. Why don't you send me more detail about the training that I can read first?"

James: "Sure, I'll get that to you tomorrow. Can I reach out to you next week to set up another session?"

Alys: "Let me get back to you."

Questions:

- How do you think James is doing?
- What isn't going well?
- How could James have done this differently?
- Have you taken the same approach as James by going into first meetings and presenting your deck?

The Product-Sales Approach

A major TRACOM client shared a story about his first job after college and military service. It was with IBM. The last part of his training was a two-week Sales School. It involved multiple role plays and lectures and was highly competitive and stressful.

He was taught a Product-Sales approach. The timeframe was after IBM transitioned from selling punch card equipment to computers. Another name for the Product-Sales approach was "speeds and feeds" going back to the punch-card era.

This approach started with what was called the Initial Benefits Statement (IBS). Here's an example: "Mr. Prospect, the reason that I'm here is that IBM has helped lots of other companies similar to yours and we believe we can also help you."

The next part of the pitch was to go into the features,

advantages, and benefits of the computer solution. "Our new computer can do 800 calculations per second with perfect accuracy and print 10,000 bills per hour." This is the "speeds and feeds part." He would then go into what this computer power could mean for the prospect. "The benefit is that we can reduce manual billing costs and produce bills earlier, thus receiving payments faster."

The Product-Sales approach works best for commodities and mass marketing. An example of someone who excels at this would have been Steve Jobs: Go back and watch an old Steve Jobs video of a new product launch. Apple stills employs this tactic today.

With the right product or service, and the application of SOCIAL STYLEs, Product-Sales methods can still be effective. It requires being adaptive enough to tailor this method to the preferences of the client rather than using a "canned" sales dialogue.

The EMAX meeting between James and Alys essentially illustrates a Product-Sales approach.

Most astoundingly, this approach is what most people use in industries such as consulting, technology, and law firms. It has a very poor success rate.

Let's do the EMAX meeting another way and see what happens.

Rewind: The EMAX Meeting Done in a Different Way

James: "Alys, I appreciate you seeing me. I would love to hear more about your organization and your role."

Alys: "Thanks James, what would you like to know?"

James: "Well, I've done some research and would like to verify that you have revenues of a bit over $11 billion and have over 100,000 employees—am I in the ballpark?"

Alys: "You are."

James: "I understand that you're the Global Managing Partner for Sales and Marketing, am I correct?"

Alys: "You are."

James: "Can you tell me your responsibilities?"

Alys: "Sure." (She then goes on to describe her responsibilities as the Global Managing Partner for Sales and Marketing.)

James: "May I ask what percentage of your revenue goes into business development or sales?"

Alys: "I have a report from our CRM system that shows that we are investing 8 percent in what we call BD."

James: "Has it always been at that level?"

Alys: "No, as a matter of fact, it had been at 6.2 percent for several years."

James: "Do you know why?"

Alys: "We are spending more and winning less these days."

James: "I assume that your CRM tells you your competitive win rate?"

Alys: "It does; we are currently at 28 percent."

James: "In my experience, that's too low. Has it always been that low?"

Alys: "No, in the past it's been around 42 percent."

James: "How much lost revenue does this represent?"

Alys: "Well, 50 percent of our revenue is sole source and/or extensions, so our competitive channel is the other half. So, increasing our competitive win rate would increase our overall revenue by billions."

James: "To what do you attribute this drop in your competitive win rate? Have you done win-loss reviews?"

Alys: "Indeed we have. Prospective clients tell us several reasons for not selecting us, including a lack of effort to build and maintain relationships—for example, they say, we never hear from you unless there is a transaction! They also say that our people are always in sales mode and don't take the time to listen, and finally, that they are poorly prepared for presentations."

Questions:

- How do you think this is going?
- Why might it be going the way it is?
- What is different from the first scenario?

This rewind demonstrates what is referred to as Adaptive Selling using a Consultative Selling approach. It's all about the client and not about you. Since James approached Alys in a way that reflects her SOCIAL STYLE, we refer to this as Adaptive Selling.

In the first example, James was all about himself and his deck. He was also insensitive to Alys' Style need by pressuring her. If Alys was another Style, James would have needed to adjust his approach in order to have the highest likelihood of success.

Solution Selling and SOCIAL STYLEs = Adaptive Selling

The person who started the Solution Selling technique was Frank Watts in 1975 during his time with Wang Labs. The company who made this technique most famous is the Huthwaite Organization started by Neil Rackham. It has since been expanded or modified by such companies as Miller Heiman, Richardson, Rain Group, and Challenger Selling.

Huthwaite and Rackham did extensive research on sales techniques at several large sales-focused companies such as IBM and Xerox. They observed that the most successful sales people asked more questions and probed deeper than others. Rackham went on to author several books on a technique he called SPIN. This acronym stands for Situation, Problem, Implication, Need/Payoff.

SPIN is a process in which you proceed through four different types of questions:

- **S** means situational questions.
- **P** means problem-focused questions.
- **I** refers to questions on the implications of the problems.
- **N** is for questions related to perceived needs and the payoffs for resolving the situation.

SPIN thus provides a systematic way of connecting with most clients.

Another example of this would be going to a doctor's office while not feeling well. Suppose the doctor says, "Let me write you a prescription to make you feel better. Also, you look overweight, and you probably have high cholesterol, so let me give you something for that as well." All of this with no questions or examination. How would you feel about that? Probably the same way your clients feel: not understood.

An excellent doctor would ask lots of questions and run tests before prescribing solutions. It's the same with great sales people. The greatest sales people take the time to understand their clients' needs and help satisfy them.

Adaptive Selling adds the use of SOCIAL STYLEs to this or any of the other sales methodologies and allows sales professionals to tailor these processes to the preferences of the client. Doing this greatly increases the probability of success regardless of the sales methodology.

It can be difficult for the Driving and Expressive Styles to be solution sellers simply because their natural tendency is to tell and not ask. These two Styles can also have problems listening. However, Expressive Style individuals who have learned to ask, listen, and probe can get great results. And they have a slight advantage over the Driving Style because they are more people-oriented. All Styles can be successful sales people, but the common characteristic is high Versatility.

The sample meetings presented earlier feature an Analytical Style client, Alys, who welcomes Jack for trying to understand her and her situation. If Alys was an Expressive and Amiable Style client she would also respond in this way. However, if she was a Driving Style client she would likely push back on the traditional Solution Selling approach unless Adaptive Selling is added to the interaction.

Using the Adaptive Selling Approach with the Driving Style

The Driving Style can become impatient during the first part of the traditional Solution Selling approach, especially when you're discussing their situation or talking about their problems. Why?

The Driving Style may feel that talking about their situation and problems is a waste of time, because they already recognize their problems. They may also wonder if you have done your homework.

We were in a meeting once where we started our presentation with a detailed discussion of the client's situation as we saw it. After several slides showing our brilliant observations, the senior executive, who was obviously a Driving Style, interrupted and said: "Folks, you have just spent 15 minutes telling us what we already know, so let's get to the point!"

So, how do you handle meetings with the Driving Style?

One way is to speed up the situational questions and get right to asking about their problems. If they push back, you may earn their respect by saying that you need to clearly understand these problems and how they rank them before you can offer any ideas.

A second way is to start by saying something such as:

"We have seen the following problems and challenges at other companies similar to yours. How true are these for you? How would you prioritize them?"

What if you are asked to come in and present your credentials?

Quite often you may be asked to come in to present credentials. The requesting organization may say that they may be interested in working with your organization in the future. Or it could be them wanting some free entertainment or education.

The tendency is to put together the credentials deck. Do so, but don't get married to it yet; it's only a draft of what you could potentially cover.

Try to arrange to interview several key members of the audience to learn their current situation and issues. Ask who will be there. Try to estimate their SOCIAL STYLEs as shown earlier. Also ask what sorts of questions could be asked.

If you have time, it is beneficial to prepare in the following way:

Create a deck that is Style-neutral. The first section should be your understanding of their situation which pleases everyone but can bore the Driving Style. As a part of your understanding of their situation, add a section on implications. This can get the Driving Style's attention.

Next, list the typical problems and opportunities that you have seen elsewhere or that you have picked up from your interview. Confirm which ones are relevant and ask them to prioritize.

You may want to list these on a flip chart and asked people to come forward and check the top three that they feel are most important. As a result, you will be able to clearly show which issues to focus on during your presentation.

Next, proceed to discuss the impacts and implications of these problems. By now, you haven't shown them anything in the way of solutions. Now take a break and rearrange the deck to address what you've learned. In all likelihood you will narrow your focus and will toss a lot of content.

What if you're asked to showcase a new product or offering to a client?

Often, large organizations may pressure sales people to bring new products and offerings to clients. If this is the case, the organization likely will have a polished deck of facts and pitches ready to go. The danger in this typical kind of attitude and preparation is that it will result in a Product-Sales attempt which very often yields nothing more than a polite "thank-you" from the client. When asked what they thought, you likely will hear, "It was interesting, but doesn't apply to us."

Before falling into this trap, follow the Adaptive Selling approach by first trying to set up interviews beforehand and starting the presentation in the same way as described above. Modify your approach based on what you learn about the SOCIAL STYLEs of the client group.

The Adaptive Selling approach applies to all stages of the deal but especially to "Discover and Connect."

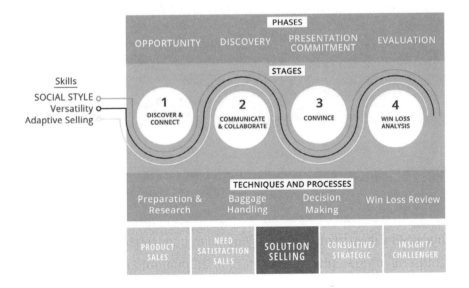

Example of a Great Solution Sale

A colleague of ours was doing a training session for a large commercial real estate company in New York City. In asking about the audience, she was told there were several folks in the audience who had made over $10 million the prior year with one having made over $20 million! She was a bit fearful of what they thought about Adaptive Selling.

After describing the technique, she asked the audience what they thought. The $20 million person answered with the following story:

She said that she had been assigned to respond to an RFP for a large auction house who was looking for a new showroom. She called them to tell them how delighted she was with the opportunity. Next, she said that she wished to visit with them to understand them better because the two organizations had never worked together. They pushed back but she convinced them that they would benefit by receiving a better proposal.

During the visit, she discovered that security of their works of art was paramount, although this wasn't obvious from the RFP. After hearing this, she found a prestigious building that had a large steel door with a driveway entrance. This building also had a great site for the auction showroom. She ended up proposing this venue and won the deal, because the new client said: "You took the time to really understand our needs. Your competitors proposed sites where we would have unloaded our priceless art works on the streets of Manhattan.

Unconscious Biases to Solution Development

As we saw earlier, cognitive biases create limitations to becoming skilled at Adaptive Selling. These biases also carry over into the realm of solution development where client needs require solutions that can't be met by standard product features and benefits. It requires sales professionals to be agile.

The importance of creating new concepts and ways of doing things has never been clearer in our global competitive marketplace. The modern era demands agility from individuals and organizations in order to survive and prosper. But our ability to be agile is affected by the Tunnel-Vision Bias, which causes us to focus on narrow goals and priorities, missing other possibilities and opportunities. We're reluctant to consider alternatives to our line of thinking, or are so focused on what we think is the correct approach that we shut ourselves off to different ways of solving problems. The consequence of this bias is we miss opportunities where we might gain a competitive advantage by considering new ways our products or services can be adapted to help clients meet their goals.

Breaking the Tunnel-Vision Bias can be achieved through strategies to enhance experimentation and openness in how to provide a solution that gives you a competitive advantage. As an example, idea-generation strategies require people to think of unusual ideas that may, at first, seem awful. The bad ideas themselves won't work; however, bad ideas often contain the roots of good ideas, so this technique forces a subtle behavior change that overcomes the Tunnel-Vision Bias. TRACOM refers to this as the "Worst Idea Strategy." People become comfortable with experimentation, risk, and ambiguity. This, in turn, helps sales teams by giving people the tools they need to be more inventive and influential in resolving client needs or taking advantage of unique opportunities. And these also allow one to be more open to unique ideas and perspectives, to changing processes and procedures, and to viewing markets and customers through different lenses.

One use of the Worst Idea Strategy occurred with a firm that was invited to respond to an RFP from a company in a market sector in which the firm had no experience. The sales team struggled with why they should even bother to respond since there were many other qualified bidders with sector experience. Someone threw out a side comment to tell the prospect they should pick them because they had no experience, no clients to reference and no similar work to show they would be any good at it. After a good laugh, they realized it might work. They bid the job with the value proposition that because they had no clients or experience in this sector, the client would be their most important client, would get the firm's best people and the firm would make sure the client was 100 percent satisfied. As a result, the firm won the RFP. At the win-loss review this innovative strategy was cited by the client as one of the primary reasons the firm won the contract.

Another organization was faced with the challenge of rapidly growing their revenues and client-base over an eighteen month period. The original plan was to invest heavily in recruiting a large sales team, spend several months training them, and then begin to try and gain new sales and customers. One of the executives who realized the difficulties of recruiting, selecting, hiring, on-boarding, and training new sales people joked that "it would be cheaper to hire customers!" This led to the idea to use the monies they would have invested in sales people to instead offer prospective clients an opportunity to try their services at no cost on a small project. The result was these free projects led to positive results for the customers and significant revenue growth and an expanded business pipeline that moved the company toward its growth targets.

SCREAM!

When exploring sales opportunities that require something beyond a standard solution we tend to think this kind of innovation is something other people do! Most of us think we should start by establishing a well-defined problem and then generate solutions with a specialist. However, another tactic is to work in the other direction—take a solution you have and find a problem it can solve. Psychologist Ronald Finke found that people are better at starting with the solution and finding problems that it can solve rather than at starting with the problem and determining a solution. For example, imagine an ice cube made out of coffee. What might be the benefits of this solution? Well, you could stick it in your iced coffee and when the ice cube melts, it will no longer dilute your drink. Now, imagine you were asked the opposite question: How do you make sure that your iced coffee doesn't get watered down over time? This is a much harder question to answer.

Adding Value by Learning to SCREAM

To become a more valued partner with your clients, you will need to overcome the cognitive biases that hold you back from finding innovative ways to create a new configuration for an existing process, product, or service that will meet the client's need. A simple but powerful strategy to find new ways of adding value from your products or service is to utilize the SCREAM strategy that TRACOM uses in its Agility training. SCREAM is an easy-to-remember acronym that can help you find and present powerful solutions to your clients. Here is a quick summary of the elements of SCREAM:

- **Substitute** — Remove integral elements of the product or service and substitute them with something else.

- **Combine** — Combine two products, two purposes or objectives, or two resources.

- **Reverse** — Reverse the process or do the opposite of what you are doing now.

- **Eliminate** — Remove certain elements of a product or service.

- **Adapt** — Adapt or adjust this product or service to achieve a different purpose or use.

- **Magnify** — Magnify or exaggerate certain elements of a product or service.

A consumer products company wanted to launch a new dental product to a major retailer and the sales team was trying to figure out how to get the client excited about adding the new product to their stores. They applied the SCREAM Strategy "Combine." They started the presentation by having the client enjoy some ice cream while the sales team showed the business case for adding the product. As the presentation went on, each client team member was given a cup of hot coffee or tea and several of them developed the type of dental pain the new product was designed to overcome. By "Combining" the business case with actual first-hand experience, the sales team was able to get their product launch.

The SCREAM Strategy "Reverse" was used when a client, who was under pressure to reduce expenditures, attempted to get a firm to lower their costs, thereby shrinking their margins. Rather than give in, the firm convinced their client to price out the project work using internal resources. The client quickly discovered that their internal costs were much greater than those of the outside firm. As a result, the client realized the firm's costs were fair and did not force them to lower their margins. This was reversing the process.

Baggage Handling

Many types of organizations, such as consulting and technology firms, bring massive change to their clients. After all, they have been hired to do so: The hiring organization may have neither the time nor the available talent to make these changes themselves. However, change-making from the outside can create relationship problems. This creates what is commonly called "Baggage" in the United States and United Kingdom.

Let's set up an example and demonstrate a first attempt at "handling" baggage.

Robert has finally been promoted to Head of Procurement of a global energy company. His promotion had been deferred because of a project that had gone badly several years ago with a leading consulting company he had hired. As part of that project, Robert had attempted to consolidate procurement world-wide. At that time, procurement had been decentralized globally. Robert is a strong Expressive Style. Robert's boss had told him that he was sure that the project would be approved and that he would receive a new promotion and title with an accompanying 40 percent raise. Hearing this, Robert promptly bought a new, expensive home with a big mortgage. He and his wife also enrolled their children in a pricey private school.

The project team, including the people from the consulting company, developed a solid business case for centralization and standardization. Unfortunately, heads of the company's Executive Leadership Team ridiculed Robert's ideas during his presentation. The geographies won, wanting to keep control of the function. Moreover, Robert couldn't answer many of the details of the business case.

After six years, however, the firm promoted Robert to Global Head of Procurement and gave him authority to centralize. Robert knew that he needed help in doing this, so he talked with several firms, including the consulting firm he had used in the past.

Sarah is a member of that consulting firm that Robert had used before. However, she was not involved in the debacle. Sarah has been assigned to respond to an RFP from the newly promoted Robert who is now a key executive. She is aware of the problematic engagement from years ago, but believes that all should be forgotten by now. Her firm has the highest ranking in procurement consulting and exceptional credentials. She has a Driving Style. She looks forward to introducing herself to Robert, whom she has determined to be an Expressive Style.

Baggage Handling Example 1

Sarah is ushered into Robert's office. After a few pleasantries, this exchange occurs.

Robert: "Well, it's about time someone showed up from your organization! I congratulate you on your courage to see me."

Sarah, somewhat taken aback: "Thank you. I want to first congratulate you on your promotion and to tell you about how excited we are with this opportunity!"

Robert, with some heat: "I would have had this job six years ago if your organization had done a proper job!"

Sarah: "I did hear that there was a problem engagement many years ago, but I'm assuming we are past that now?"

Robert: "You may be, but I'm not. You have no idea what you did to me."

Sarah: "Really?"

Robert: "Your firm did a terrible job. You put together a business case that I couldn't defend. You also didn't go around and pre-sell the business case to our executive team. In addition, you didn't prepare me properly for their tough questions! You can't imagine how embarrassed I was and how this impacted me personally."

Sarah: "I'm sorry to hear that but let me assure you that we won't make the same mistake again."

Robert: "Sure, I'll bet. Did you know that if my vision for consolidation had gone through, I would have been promoted on the spot with a huge compensation increase?"

Sarah: "I didn't."

Robert: "Well, you should. Let me tell you how much this has hurt me. When my boss said that he was sure that the project would be approved and that I would be promoted, my wife and I bought a large house with a huge mortgage. We also enrolled our two children in an expensive private school. We had to borrow money from my mother-in-law to survive."

Sarah: "What would you suggest to us to avoid a disaster again?"

Robert: "Aren't you the consultant that should know how to handle this sort of thing? Why are you asking me?"

> How do you think this one is going?
> What might you have done differently?

Baggage Handling Example 2

Sarah is ushered into Robert's office. After a few pleasantries, this follows.

Robert: "Well, it's about time someone showed up from your organization! I congratulate you on your courage to see me."

Sarah, somewhat taken aback: "Wow, sounds like you are upset."

Robert: "You are darn right that I am upset. Do you know how your firm almost ruined my career?"

Sarah: "I'm sorry to hear that. Can you tell me what happened?"

Robert: "Your firm did a terrible job for me. You put together a business case that I couldn't defend. You also didn't go around and pre-sell this to our executive team. And then you didn't prepare me properly for their tough questions! You can't image how embarrassed I was and how this impacted me personally."

Sarah: "I can image how it would be so embarrassing. Tell me how it impacted you personally."

Robert: "Did you know that if the deal had gone through, I would have been promoted to the job I have now with a huge compensation increase?"

Sarah: "I didn't, but not getting the recognition and a raise would certainly be painful."

Robert: "Let me tell you again how much this has hurt me. When my boss said that he was sure that the project would be approved and that I would be promoted, my wife and I bought a large house with a huge mortgage. We also enrolled our two children in an expensive private school. We had to borrow money from my mother-in-law to survive."

Sarah: "That's horrible! You've been though a lot!"

Robert, starting to settle down: "I have been."

Sarah: "It hurts me to see what you have been through."

> How's this one going?
> What makes it better than the one before?

Baggage Handling and Empathy

In the second meeting, Sarah is displaying empathy. So, what is empathy? Empathy is <u>understanding</u> and <u>acknowledging</u> the other person's feelings. In the first meeting, Sarah certainly understood that Robert was upset, but she never acknowledged his feelings. Instead, she wanted to flee!

Not acknowledging feelings is the big miss. How do you acknowledge these feelings? Hopefully, your body language and facial expressions show compassion toward what you are hearing, but that is not enough. You need to make empathy statements. In the second example, Sarah's empathy statements were:

- "Wow, sounds like you are upset."

- "I'm sorry to hear that. Can you tell me what happened?"

- "I can imagine why that would be so embarrassing. Tell me how it impacted you personally."

- "I didn't, but not getting the recognition and a raise would certainly be painful."

- "That's horrible! You've been though a lot!"

There is an academic debate about empathy. Some believe that you can only be truly empathetic if you feel that same way. Others believe that you don't have to necessarily feel that same way, but instead you need to feel a sense of compassion at seeing them in such a state. This is the most common view of empathy.

Frequently, some describe the angry person as being in the "House of Pain" that may have many rooms. The angry person may want you to go into all of them in order to calm things down. Sarah showed her willingness to do this with these statements:

- "Can you tell me what happened?"

- "Tell me how it impacted you personally."

Unfortunately, the normal way the role play goes is that there is no empathy. What happens is what is called a two-house meeting. The client sits inside the first house, or the "House of Pain," while the consultant wants to move to the second house, or the "Solution Center."

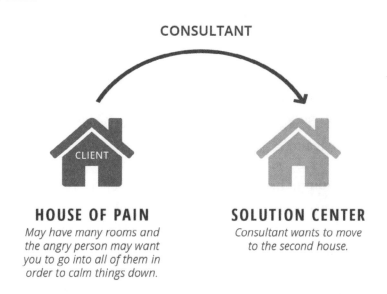

CONSULTANT

HOUSE OF PAIN
May have many rooms and the angry person may want you to go into all of them in order to calm things down.

CLIENT

SOLUTION CENTER
Consultant wants to move to the second house.

We will need to stay in the House of Pain as long as it is necessary. Sometimes we will be stuck here for just a few minutes; other times, it may take several calls.

The SOCIAL STYLE of the client in the interaction will impact both the time required and the approach used. Sometimes we may be stuck here indefinitely and can never jettison the baggage.

Sarah also did something else to connect with Robert. Here are her words:

"It hurts me to see what you have been through."

With this comment, Sarah shows her feelings in a sincere way. Again, this can help connect and start a relationship. Note that this doesn't mean that Sarah necessarily agrees with Robert's feelings, but she is genuinely upset that he is distressed.

There are several other mistakes to avoid:

- **Re-assuring too quickly:** Sarah did this in the first example by saying, "I'm sorry to hear that, but let me *assure* you that we won't make the same mistake again." It may be fine to assure late in the dialogue if you have settled things down.

- **Asking the client to fix the issue:** In the first meeting, Sarah tried this with alarming results and made Robert even more angry. She said, *"How would you suggest* that we avoid disaster again?"

- **Defending:** Imagine how much worse the first meeting would have gone if Sarah had said something like, "I learned that we actually had offered to visit with key executives before the meeting, but you declined this idea."

- **Fixing too quickly:** This is where you want to get over to the Solution Center as soon as you can. You simply can't do this until the heat is lowered.

- **Expressing culpability:** In an attempt to move to the Solution Center, many accept fault and blame for the problem. "Well, we weren't at our best then," for example. The problem with doing this is that Robert could then say, "So you accept that your firm did a bad job? Then I want my money back!"

Baggage Handling and SOCIAL STYLEs

If we are of the Driving or Analytical Styles, we may find it challenging to act as the exorcist in these sorts of conversations. Conversations about feelings don't come naturally to us, nor does using words that describe feelings. Moreover, Driving Styles tend to want to fix things quickly.

The Driving and Analytical Styles need to be versatile when dealing with baggage. This Versatility comes more easily for Amiable and Expressive Styles, though Expressive people may need to tone down their tendency to talk and not listen and probe.

What about the upset person? How could we restructure the baggage exorcism to cater to each of the different Styles?

Amiable and Expressive Styles express their feelings more readily so we must make sure that we acknowledge these feelings quickly. The Driving and Analytical Styles don't readily use feeling words and don't show their emotions as much. They still have feelings though.

If Robert had been a Driving or an Analytical Style, he would have been more factual in his remarks such as, "We invested $1.3 million with you in the centralization project. It took five months. We developed a solid business case with a 2.1-year payback. Your people did a poor job of pre-selling this to key executives, and they killed the plan to protect their own interests."

"My boss promised me a promotion to Global Head of Procurement that would have resulted in a 40 percent raise. Based on this, my wife purchased an expensive home and enrolled our children in a private school that my take-home pay couldn't cover. We've had to borrow over $200,000 from my mother-in-law as a result."

Note that no feeling words were used. For example, nothing was said about hurt or embarrassment, for example. Robert still had those feelings, though.

When performing a baggage-exorcism meeting with a Driving or Analytical Style, interject feeling words for them. For example, after the line about the plan being killed, you could say, "That was probably embarrassing for you." Or, "I can imagine you are still upset about this today." Quite likely, they will say that you are right and you will have made a connection.

Another point is that the Driving Style may want to go to your Solution Center too early. Try to stay in their House of Pain to make sure that you understand as many of their feelings as you can.

We can't go around always looking to have empathetic conversations, though. In other words, you don't want to be the person whose shoulder everyone cries on. Baggage exorcism exhausts the exorcist, making you less productive in the remainder of your job. Also, other team members may believe that you spend too much time with the complainers.

Example of a Great Empathy Sale

An attorney was asked to visit the CEO of large and well-known company who was being battered at the time due to recent indiscretions. The attorney arrived, and was the last person the CEO would see after a terrible week of negative publicity surrounding potential civil and criminal charges.

The attorney arrived with a briefcase of relevant case studies, proven best practices for this type of situation, and endorsements from other clients.

The CEO was slumped over, looking almost physically battered when the attorney walked in. The attorney sat down and said: "If you don't mind me saying so, you look like you have been beaten up."

The CEO said: "Yes, that's right. The press attacks me every day, plus politicians are constantly trying to ruin me."

The attorney said: "This must be difficult. Not only for you, but for your family."

The conversation stayed in the House of Pain for a long time and the attorney won the engagement from the CEO because of his exceptional empathic skills.

Baggage Handling and Empathic Skills and Stages of a Sales Cycle

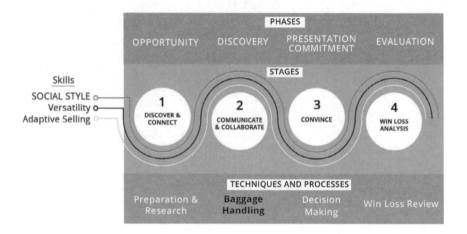

One of the things that interests top sales professionals is how decisions are made, especially those involving lots of money. This interest was made popular by a 1985 book, Strategic Selling by Robert Miller and Stephen Heiman, which introduced the concept of Decision Mapping.

Miller and Heiman's book charged into sales-oriented companies like IBM and Hewlett Packard. It seemed that every professional had this book on his or her bookshelf. At TRACOM, we have leaned toward the Power Mapping concept but wanted to simplify it while combining it with SOCIAL STYLEs. The result is what we refer to as Decision Mapping and is an element of Adaptive Selling.

Decision Mapping analyzes how decisions are made. It shows **who** is involved, what their role is, and how they **influence** each other. Obviously, this concept applies to many situations, not just sales.

Let's start with the description of the key players:

• **Evaluators** evaluate. They meet with bidders and sometimes read and grade proposals. They may attend final presentations. Evaluators may evaluate only certain parts of a bid. For example, in a commercial-construction bid, certain evaluators may only evaluate HVAC, while others manage interior design, security, and so on.

• **Recommenders** provide the recommendation for approvals. They do so by looking at what evaluators say. Quite possibly the HVAC team in the construction bid may prefer one bid, and the interior design evaluators prefer another. The recommenders have to sort this out.

• **Approvers** either approve, disapprove, or put off the decision. Normally they approve what is recommended, making Recommenders the most important of the three.

A person can perform all of these roles. The larger the deal, the more people involved. It is rare to have just one person serve as all three. Thus, there is a dislike for the inappropriate question: "who's the real decision maker?" The answer is that the decision is more likely to go up through these sets of people. Certainly, some people may have more influence in the decision than others, as will be described shortly.

There are two other roles—**Influencers** and **Coaches**. Influencers are people who may be within the organization or even outside who can be influencing the three players above. Of course, Evaluators, Recommenders, and Approvers can influence each other as we will explore.

Key players may also be classified as **Coaches**. Coaches help you in the buying process by telling you where you are strong, where you are weak, who your supporters are, and who your competition is. They can also tell you about how the key players are influencing each other. Coaches normally come from those who are also Evaluators, Recommenders, or Approvers as well as Influencers.

A Powerful Story About the Importance of Coaches

A senior executive at a consulting firm received an RFP from a company where the consulting firm had never worked. Of course, the opportunity to break into this company was exciting, but the senior consulting executive worried about the chances of winning plus the cost of proposing and wondered if his firm was just being used as a "stalking horse."

After research, the consulting firm found that a respected competitor had been working with the firm for quite a while. He arranged a meeting with the sponsoring executive at the target in order to decide on whether or not to bid.

The consulting firm executive shared his concerns with the target executive and wondered why they would bring in someone else, especially if the competitor was doing good work. The target company executive said that the incumbent was doing a decent job, but that he felt that they were not paying enough attention to him and his company. The consulting executive noted that the executive was an Expressive Style, and he knew that he could be turned because of the low loyalty of Expressive people. The consulting executive said that to bid, he needed coaches within the target to tell his team how they were doing.

The target company's sponsoring executive said that he would be a coach. The consulting executive responded positively, but said that he would also need someone on the ground who would be extremely close to the evaluation on a daily basis. The target company agreed and assigned a coach to the new bidder.

The consulting firm won because of their boldness and also knowing that the Expressive Style has a low loyalty and responds well to personal attention.

To win, one really needs to have one or more coaches. You need to find them if you don't have any. The preference for Expressive-Style Coaches is that they will coach even when they prefer another bidder. The reason is that they delight in telling you what they know. In looking for coaches, start with the Expressive Style but be Versatile enough to also enlist Driving, Analytical, and Amiable Styles.

Our Decision Mapping technique also adds VIPs (Very Influential People) to the analysis. These are people who have unusual influence over everyone else. They can also be Evaluators, Recommenders, Approvers, and occasionally Influencers.

Let's now delve into this method and build a decision map:

STEP #1:

Who are the Key Players? Record the names of the people you believe are the key players within the potential client on a flip chart or whiteboard. Let's set up a fictious potential client and a sales team that is proposing to them and develop a Decision Map to see how it works.

Client Team Members:

- Samuel is the Project Lead and the company's Business Development Manager

- Harriet is the Manager of Finance

- Rachael is the Manager of Information Service

- Ruppert is the Senior Design Architect

Sales Team Members:

- Sarah is the Senior Partner responsible for the Systems Practice area and has a Driving Style

- Guy is the Senior Manager whose team will deliver the project. He has an Amiable Style.

STEP #2:

Now, for each person, identify what roles you believe they fulfill and if they are a VIP or have limited influence in the opportunity. Once this is completed, evaluate the strength of the relationship you or others in your company have with the individual. Based on that, determine which members of the client team may be a Coach for you.

For example, let's look at the roles of the Client Team members:

- Samuel is seen as having several important roles; he is the Project Lead and a Recommender, he has an Expressive Style and he agreed to be a Coach. He is a VIP because the final Decision Maker will rely strongly on Samuel's recommendation.

- Harriet is the finance person and is both a Recommender and an Influencer. She has an Analytical Style. She may also be a Coach because of the strength of the relationship you have with her.

- Rachael manages the Systems and Technology group and is an Influencer and Evaluator. She has a Driving Style and because the project you are recommending has a direct impact on her departments, she is a VIP and an Approver.

- Ruppert is the lead within the client's Development and

Systems department. This is the department that has asked you to propose a major consulting project to assist them in the creation of a new generation of applications for their markets. He is an Evaluator and a Recommender who has an Analytical Style.

STEP #3:

Let's move on to begin mapping this team. Begin by listing the names of each person on the left side of a chart. Indicate their position, roles, SOCIAL STYLE, and if they are a VIP, a key player, etc.

Samuel is the Project Lead. Project Leads, especially if they are in charge of the implementation, should normally be treated as VIP. You can also see that Samuel has been identified as a Coach, which is promising.

Relationships each Client Team Member has with your team and your competitor are shown on the right. Relationships are graded from A to F.

For Samuel you judge the relationship with you as an "A" while you believe your competitor only has a "C" relationship.

In judging relationships, an "A" is the best. We define an "A" as being someone you can call at home on the weekend. You have both a personal and business relationship. A "B" relationship is a great business relationship only. A "C" is an average business relationship based on limited interactions. A "D" is a poor business relationship that can potentially be repaired if the reason is identified. An "F" relationship is one so bad that it's beyond repair.

Now let's continue mapping the Client Team.

With Harriett you have an "A" relationship with her but you do not know about her relationship with the competitor so you rated it a "C."

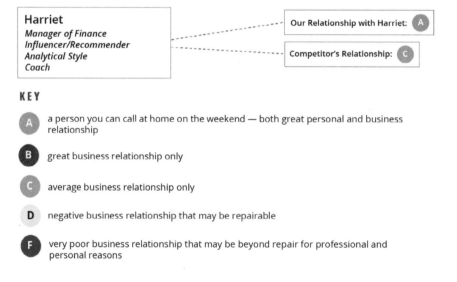

Your relationship with Rachael is also a "C" and she has an "A" relationship with the competitor.

Rachael

Manager of Information Services
Evaluator/Influencer/Approver
Driving Style

Our Relationship with Rachael: C

Competitor's Relationship: A

KEY

A   a person you can call at home on the weekend — both great personal and business relationship

B   great business relationship only

C   average business relationship only

D   negative business relationship that may be repairable

F   very poor business relationship that may be beyond repair for professional and personal reasons

With Ruppert you have a "D" relationship and you think he has a "C" relationship with the competitor.

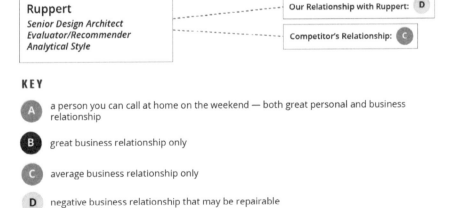

Ruppert

Senior Design Architect
Evaluator/Recommender
Analytical Style

Our Relationship with Ruppert: D

Competitor's Relationship: C

KEY

A   a person you can call at home on the weekend — both great personal and business relationship

B   great business relationship only

C   average business relationship only

D   negative business relationship that may be repairable

F   very poor business relationship that may be beyond repair for professional and personal reasons

This data should allow you to map a chart like the following:

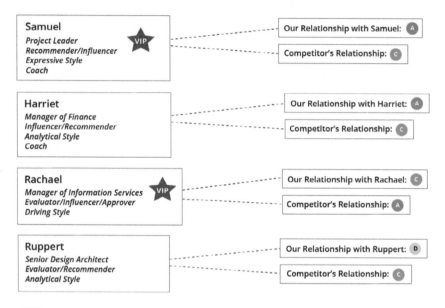

KEY

A a person you can call at home on the weekend — both great personal and business relationship

B great business relationship only

C average business relationship only

D negative business relationship that may be repairable

F very poor business relationship that may be beyond repair for professional and personal reasons

STEP #4:

The next step is to overlay all the players players on the Social-Style grid as shown.

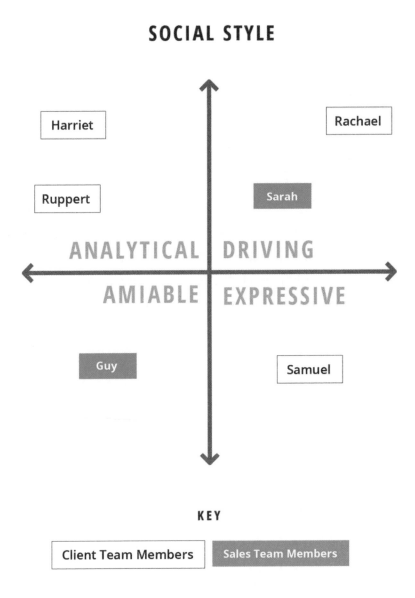

SOCIAL STYLE

Decision Mapping

Now you can see where both the Client Team Members and the Sales Team Members fall in terms of their behavioral style. The next step is to rate each Client Team Member in terms of your and your competitor's Strength of Relationship from "A" to "F."

When mapping, record an "A" relationship on your chart with GREEN, show "B" in PURPLE, show "C" in LIGHT BLUE, show "D" in YELLOW and show "F" in RED. For your competitor's relationships with the Client Team you can simply add a small dot or check-mark next to the client's name that is in the color that reflects what you believe is the relationship rating for that person with the competitor. For example, Samuel has a GREEN "A" next to his name in the Expressive Style position which indicates our "A" relationship with him. You would then put a LIGHT BLUE dot or check-mark next to his name to show your competitor's "C" Strength of Relationship with Samuel. For Rachael you would put a LIGHT BLUE "C" to show your relationship with her and a GREEN dot to show the "A" relationship she has with the competitor. Your other "A" relationship is Harriett which you would show in GREEN while there would be LIGHT BLUE dot for the competitor since that relationship is not fully known. Finally, Ruppert would have an YELLOW "D" for your relationship and a LIGHT BLUE dot to indicate his relationship with the competitor.

SAMPLE DECISION MAP

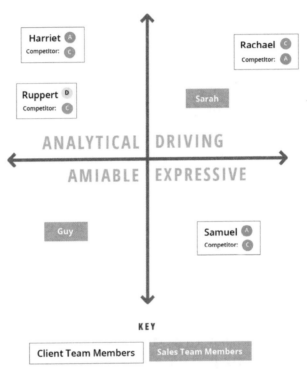

KEY

| Client Team Members | Sales Team Members |

A a person you can call at home on the weekend — both great personal and business relationship

B great business relationship only

C average business relationship only

D negative business relationship that may be repairable

F very poor business relationship that may be beyond repair for professional and personal reasons

STEP #5:

This step adds an important addition to the Decision Map which is the influence lines.

• The lines show how the key players influence each other. The thicker the line, then the stronger the influence.

• Thick BLUE lines indicate a Strong Influence, thin BLUE lines indicate Moderate Influence, etc.

• Dotted BLACK Lines indicate slight influence on someone. For example, in the chart Harriett and Ruppert both influence each other strongly (thick BLUE line) whereas Rachael influences Samuel only a little (dotted BLACK line)

• These influence lines are determined by the relationship, connections, and by position in the hierarchy.

• A RED line shows a negative relationship. Here we can see that Harriett and Rachael don't get along.

• The Light Blue lines are from the selling team to the buyers and their thickness shows the strength of the relationship.

SAMPLE DECISION MAP

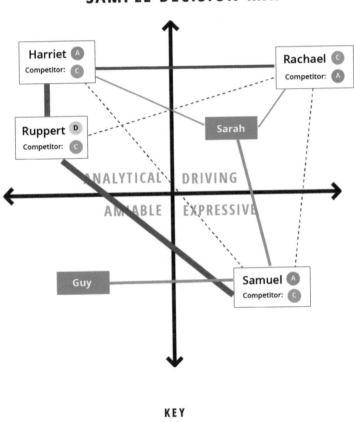

KEY

▬ Strong Influence		▬ Selling team to buyers	
--- Moderate Influence		▬ Negative Relationship	

How to Interpret a Decision Map and Then Use It to Guide Your Strategy and Tactics

We recommend that you go through the following steps:

- First, look at your relationships and ask where you are strong and where you are weak. Looking at the Decision Map in the example, the Sales Team is strong with Harriett and Samuel, neutral with Rachael, and poor with Ruppert.

- Ask if you have any coaches. In the example you have one, Samuel. It would be beneficial to have more. We would recommend trying Harriett because of your "A" quality relationship.

- Next, consider your strengths according to the Decision Map. The Sales Team in the example should feel good about their "A" relationships with Harriet and Samuel. Samuel is especially good to have on their side because he is the project lead and an Alpha Dog.

- They should also feel good about Harriet, because she is an Analytical person who has had exceptional influence during the final stages of previous deals. This influence is because frequently the Analytical Styles are thorough and fact-based. Another good thing is that Harriet, being an Analytical Style, will be loyal. A final slight feel-good is Sarah's slightly positive relationship with Rachael, although the relationship holds room for improvement.

- What should worry the Sales Team first is Ruppert's "D" relationship with them and his strong influence over Samuel.

Also worrisome is Rachael's "C" relationship with the Sales Team as contrasted with her "A" relationship with the competitor since she is an Evaluator/Recommender and has some possible Approver role. Lastly, we should worry about losing Samuel from our camp, because of the Expressive Style's known shifting loyalties.

Next Steps for success in the example:

• Keep Samuel, an Expressive Style and a Very Influential Person (VIP), on board by focusing lots of attention toward him. Bring in the senior executives to meet him to tell him how excited they are about his vision.

• Try to turn Ruppert around. Something happened to make him negative. No one on the sales team has a relationship with him. A "Baggage Exorcism" meeting may be necessary. Also, try to get Harriet to help us because she has a strong influence over Ruppert.

• We also need to work on Rachael. She needs more confidence in us. She currently doesn't feel good enough about our ability to deliver the results she wants. Put highly credible people in front of her.

You can now see the utility of a Decision Map. It is the dashboard for a deal. In sketching a Decision Map, you will better understand how to proceed amongst competing webs of influence.

Another point is that there may be several Decision Maps for a deal. For a large deal with many involved, you may need a Decision Map for the Recommenders and another for the Approvers, plus individual ones for each evaluation team and one for the negotiating team. One client's deal once featured eleven Decision Maps.

Building a Decision Map

The most accurate Decision Maps are built by observing relationships and asking clarification questions when needed. In observing relationships, note who comes to meetings. Who seems the most important? How do they interact and influence each other? You can also determine their SOCIAL STYLEs from thoughtful observation or using the SOCIAL STYLE Estimator tool.

Another component of building Decision Maps is asking questions. Remember below-the-line styles like the Amiable and Expressive are likely to tell you more and generally will provide coaching, but others will **answer questions** like these below:

- How many people are involved?

- How many are reading proposals? Who are they?

- Do certain people only read and score parts of the proposal?

- Do they have a scoresheet? What are its factors? Are they weighted?

- Do the people doing evaluations take findings to another group to make a final recommendation? This will tell you the recommenders who are the most important people in the deal.

- Who are the recommenders?

- What is the SOCIAL STYLE of each person in this exclusive group? (Refer to questions from previous sections about high and low energy, emotiveness, etc. for relevant criteria.)

• What are the relationships like in the group (the Recommenders)? Or, who influences whom? Is there an Alpha Dog in this group? Who do they listen to most?

• How do these people feel about you and your proposal? Why do they feel this way?

• Do you have coaches?

• Who is uncomfortable with you or your firm? Why? How can you win them over?

• Who are your competitor's advocates?

• Are your competitors doing anything differently from you? Can you tell me what?

• What would you like to know that you don't know now?

• Are you sure that there isn't a question that you haven't asked but should? This is an amazing question that can have surprising rewards.

You may think that many of these questions are too bold, but if your relationships are strong enough, don't hesitate to ask them. Certainly those using the Challenger-Selling process would advocate direct questions. But to make sure the questions are well received, remember to build trust through behaving with Versatility. Also, a nice dinner with wonderful wines can help!

Decision Mapping and the Stages of a Deal

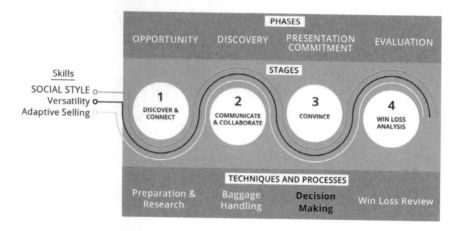

Start building your Decision Map as soon as you can, but you must have one for the Convince stage where you are "Proposing" and "Presenting."

You have now covered several concepts and skills, including:

- SOCIAL STYLEs and Versatility

- Solution Selling in its various forms

- Baggage Handling and Empathy

- Decision Mapping

There are two more topics to cover, the first being How to Prepare for Important Meetings and Presentations.

Presentations are **huge!** They are where the final decisions are most often made. You can be ahead in the deal and lose due to your poor presentations.

How to Prepare for Important Meetings and Presentations

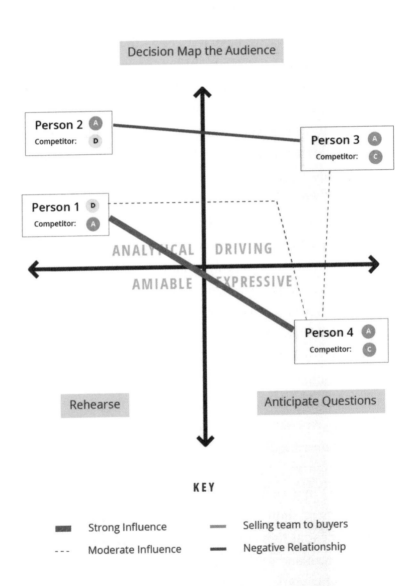

Decision Map the Audience

Person 2 (A) Competitor: (D)

Person 3 (A) Competitor: (C)

Person 1 (D) Competitor: (A)

ANALYTICAL   DRIVING
AMIABLE   EXPRESSIVE

Person 4 (A) Competitor: (C)

Rehearse

Anticipate Questions

KEY

— Strong Influence
--- Moderate Influence

— Selling team to buyers
— Negative Relationship

Decision Map the Audience

We are often asked to help prepare teams for Presentations. The first thing that we want to see is a Decision Map of the audience. Quite often, teams that we have not yet worked with didn't have a Decision Map. So, we start with: "Who's going to be in attendance from the client's team?" The team replies, "Well, we are sure that Sally, John, or Alys will be there." We then ask, "Any others?"

The team then debates whom they think could be there. We then instruct the team to call Sally, John, or Alys to inquire about the others. Suddenly Sally, John, and Alys are to be accompanied by four others, two of whom you do not know at all. When that happens, make it a priority to try to meet those two.

If you can't meet with the unknown participants, then talk with coaches to find out what you can about their SOCIAL STYLEs and relationships. Try to make a good guess at their SOCIAL STYLE using the technique described earlier.

With these steps, we can now help the team build a Decision Map and start to debate influence lines, roles, who the VIPs are, and grade relationships.

From this, they can see who they need to orient the session toward. In our experience, you seldom have the need to worry about **more** than two of the SOCIAL STYLEs. Next, you need to build your presentation and start rehearsing.

The first thing to do in building the presentation is to print the potential topics as shown in the section on "Organizing by Style." Print each potential topic on its own page, that way you can tape them all to a wall and see which potential topics you should select from and in which order.

After debating about the topics and their order, you can then decide on the media for each. For example, you can have PowerPoint slides, charts, animations, videos, and demonstrations. It is strongly recommended that you mix up your media, as many don't like "death by PowerPoint"!

It often takes six hours of preparation for every hour one plans to be in front of the client. This means that, if you have a day set aside for rehearsal, you should spend most of your time deciding on what to present, in what order, and by whom.

Rehearsals

If the quality of an unrehearsed presentation is 1x then one rehearsal will make it three times better than if you didn't rehearse at all. Another rehearsal will take it to 4x in quality compared to no rehearsal.

A common objection to rehearsing is that there is too little time or not enough financial stake in the proposal to make rehearsing worthwhile. The latter could very well be true, but definitely attempt to rehearse if the deal is important.

Let's say that you are competitively bidding for a small job for a client with whom you have never worked before. If you win and successfully deliver what they want, there could be more and bigger jobs on the horizon. Wouldn't you want to rehearse to greatly improve your chances given the long-term potential of the client?

A good best practice is to invite someone to your rehearsals from outside the team. It is ideal if this person knows the client well and is the same SOCIAL STYLE as one of the key attendees on your Decision Map.

Anticipate Questions

We have found two things from numerous Win-Loss Reviews:

the first is that if a sales person or team wins the final presentation, then they are highly likely to win the deal. The second thing is that, *when they lose in the final presentation, it is most often due to bungling answers to questions.* The lesson is that you must anticipate questions. After listing anticipated questions, assign specific individuals to answer and rehearse them. And remember to approach the answers in a manner that meets the needs of each Style!

Here are some generic questions:

- What assumptions are you making and what options have you considered?

- Tell us the risks that you see and how they will be mitigated?

- Where have you done this before and who are your best references?

- How much experience does your proposed team have?

- How will you team up with us?

- When will we see results?

- How is your organization different and why should we pick you?

- Are you the sales team or the delivery team?

- How much time will each of you here today spend with us if you win the project?

- What will the governance model look like?

- What are your greatest learnings in this area?

Every organization needs a list of probable questions. We recommend to our clients that they circulate the above list to their people and ask that they add questions that they have experienced. You soon will easily have 100 questions from which you can select the likeliest questions for each presentation or meeting.

Preparation is key to all stages, especially during the Convince stage.

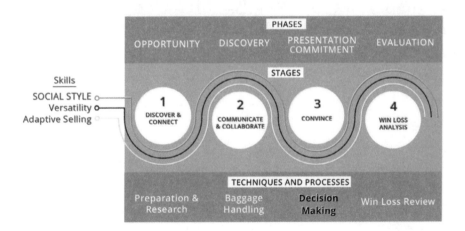

"Several years ago, I had a top sales person on my team who was meticulous at call planning and really embraced SOCIAL STYLEs as part of that prep. One of the things that she would talk about in planning the call was, 'This person is this particular Style, and I know it because I see these types of behaviors and hear this type of language.' Then, as she got into the meat of the call prep, she would lead us through a discussion. "So here's what we're trying to get across to them or ask them to do, 'Considering that this person has a Driving Style, this is probably how we ought to try to orient the conversation.' She was very thoughtful in her planning, and SOCIAL STYLE was at the core of much of her thinking. She was a strong Expressive Style, thinking about people a great deal, so using Style was just something that became very routine for her, a part of her cadence in how she prepared herself. And she had great success in her career."

— Fred Dulin
Corporate Sales Director, Eastman Chemical Company

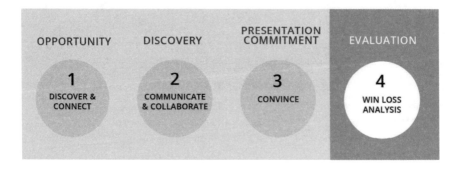

> *"In loss reviews, I have had people tell me that although the content of what they were delivering was really good, the meeting still went really bad. Now why is that? People usually say that 'it wasn't delivered in the right way...this happened, that happened, etc.' That's when they realize that it's not the material, it's not the information, it's not what they're providing but it's how it's being delivered that is making all the difference."*
>
> **— Jim Knauss II**
> **Global Markets Leader, People Advisory Services – EY**

Organizations often don't know why they win and why they lose. When we ask a losing sales team why they lost, they most often reply with something like, "Our competitor bought the business!" Price, in other words. Evidence shows that price is down the list.

We counter the price statement by asking if the client had said to them that they wanted to do business with them, but their price was out of line. If the client didn't, then you didn't lose because of pricing.

The same can be true of wins. The client often buys from you for reasons that aren't obvious, so you should try to learn these. However, you do learn more from Loss Reviews than you do from wins.

Much of what is shared in this book comes from doing hundreds of these reviews.

Here are the steps to take:

• Have someone independent from the sales team do the review. This person needs good questioning, listening, probing, and empathic skills. In losses, it is especially important to *not* let the losing team do the review. The reason is that they can make the relationship worse by going into a defensive mode, attack mode, or denial.

• Have the losing sales team write a letter to the client asking for the review. Key phrases are shown in the text box.

• Assuming that the client accepts (and they normally do), then individual interviews should be scheduled for 45 minutes each. Typically, two to four of these are enough.

> ## Sample Phrases Asking for a Loss Review:
>
> *"We are naturally disappointed in losing your business but respect your decision. We would like to learn from this so that we can better respond to you in the future. May we interview several of your people who were involved in the decision?"*

• The interviewer should first sit down with the sales team and ask their opinions on the win or loss. They should also ask what the sales team would like to know. In addition, ask or determine the Styles of the people being interviewed. It is also beneficial to have a Decision Map.

• Top loss facilitators always ask for and almost always receive permission to record interviews. This allows them to not be burdened by note taking. They can then review and transcribe or summarize the outcomes more easily. If appropriate, try to let the losing team listen to these unless the client asked you not to do so.

Sample Questions to Ask in the Interview Sessions

• Can you summarize the key points as to why we won or lost?

• I would like to ask about several things: Your selection process, who was involved, your selection criteria, what our organization did well, and where we fell short. Do you mind if we start with these?

• Ask questions about each of these. Under selection criteria, ask about weighting of the criteria. For example, if they say "cultural fit" was a factor, ask how important it was.

• When asking about the people involved, try to get enough information to draw your version of the Decision Map. Determine who the evaluators were, the recommenders, and approvers. Ask who was the most influential. Later show your Decision Map to your team and compare to theirs. This can be a great learning experience.

• You should ask specific questions based on the SOCIAL STYLE of the person you are interviewing:

■ **Questions to Analytical Styles**

- Did the team understand you well? Where you are now and where you are going?
- Did they understand the risks?
- Were they transparent?
- Were they too salesy?

■ **Questions to Driving Styles**

- Did the team understand the results you wanted to achieve?
- Were they credible?

- Did they have the experience that you wanted?

- Could they answer your questions?

▪ Questions to Expressive Styles

- Did they understand your vision?

- Were their senior executives involved?

- Were they excited about working with you?

- Did they do enough to demonstrate how their solution would be viewed across your organization?

▪ Questions to Amiable Styles

- Did you like them personally?

- Would they have fit in with your culture?

- Did they understand the people and change management risks?

- Were you comfortable with their proven experience?

These questions point to how well the team connected with and built relationships with the different people. For example, if an Analytical Style client says that your team was too pushy and salesy, then translate this into a relationship issue where there never was a connection.

Here are some other questions to ask:

• Pricing: Was your organization's bid competitive?

• If your bid was out of line, ask by how much. Also ask if

the buyer informed your organization of this. You can then ask if the client would have bought from you if the price had been the same. Most often then the answer is no.

- The Competition:

    – What did your competitor do especially well?
    – What did they do differently?
    – Were they especially creative?
    – Did they understand you better?
    – Was their solution superior?

- Finally, ask: "Is there anything that I haven't asked but should have?"

You will see patterns emerge in doing this and will learn a great deal. Now let's bring everything together to show a typical deal.

Deal-Flow Stages

This section will discuss elements of the diagram below.

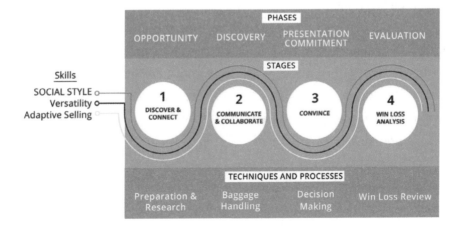

This section will add detail to the Deal-Flow Stages Model. Let's start with Opportunities.

Opportunities come from four primary sources:

- New opportunities with existing clients
- Targeting activities to potential new clients
- Bluebirds
- RFPs

Opportunities are either sole source or competitive. Sole source work can come from extensions and expansions of current work. Opportunities generated from targeting and coming from bluebirds can also be sole source. Many organizations generate more than 70 percent of their revenue as a result of sole sourcing. This reduces business development costs.

The procurement function bought pencils and paper fifty years ago. Now, they have gained stature and power and have moved well beyond commodity purchases. Larger organizations are likely to have procurement heavily involved in everything including IT and legal services. Putting more contracts out to bid is the result of procurement's involvement.

In our experience, procurement runs the buying process and tries to normalize proposals so that they can be compared. For sure you will see them on the Evaluation and Negotiating Teams but they may not be on the Recommender Team. You need to find out what role they are playing in deals, especially to see if they are Recommenders.

Highest win rates and lowest costs come from cross-selling within existing clients. With good work and good relationships, your client sponsors and coaches should be happy to take you to meet with executives where you would like to build relationships and introduce your services/solutions.

Sometimes account teams who are protective of their client and relationships push back on attempts by other members of their organization to pursue their service offerings within a client. They can block this attempt to build synergy and overall business within a client. This can be frustrating and inhibit growth.

The second source for opportunities is from **targeting new clients**. The best targets are with companies who have similar problems that you have already solved with existing clients. Most important in chasing these prospects is to first focus on confirming that they have similar problems and to start to establish a relationship.

Bluebirds fly in the window. They are opportunities that can be the result of marketing and advertising activities, publications or articles that you have written, speeches given, or internet research. It can also come from an old client moving to a new organization.

Finally, every organization receives **RFPs**. Some of these RFPs are from existing or past clients and some from potential clients with whom you haven't worked before. Win rates are higher for the first two and lower for potential clients where you have never worked before. Win rates on RFPs from existing and past clients should be 50 percent. For clients where you have never worked, you should only bid if you determine that your chances are 30 percent or higher. Your potential revenue should be at least fifteen times the cost of bidding. Other qualification factors should include the quality or absence of relationships, whether or not you can get coaching, and the client's relationships with competitors. It is recommended that you meet in person with brand new prospective clients in order to qualify them before bidding.

Discover and Connect

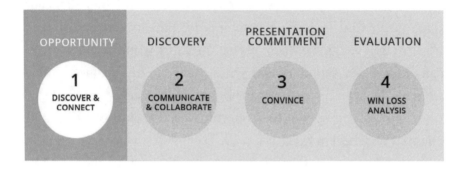

This is the second stage of a typical deal. Discover and Connect is where you take opportunities received or generated from targeting, bluebirds, or RFPs and you have decided that you will likely bid. This is where you meet with the prospect, often for the first time.

Your main objective is to learn more about the opportunity and to start or renew the relationship. You also want to start gathering information about who will be involved in the decision, their SOCIAL STYLEs, and what the Decision Map will look like. Avoid the temptation to treat these meetings as "tell and sell." You should also be qualifying in this stage and potentially not bid if the conditions do not look favorable.

Adapting to the prospect's SOCIAL STYLE, using an Adaptive Sales approach, and preparing well are the best practices to be used.

Communicate and Collaborate

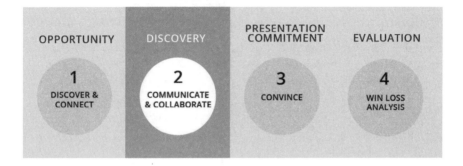

This stage is where you continue to better understand the players in the deal and what they are looking for. Also, you want to be enhancing your relationships. You still should be in "Listen and Learn" mode if you are meeting with the client.

You need to start or refine your Decision Map during this time. Also, "Baggage Exorcisms" can be done if necessary

You are also architecting your solution. You should collaborate and test this with the client, which will likely lead to refinement. In addition, you can test your people by asking the client how confident they are in the people they have met. If you see a problem, then you need to remove these players from your team.

If the deal is competitive, then you may be writing a proposal. If possible, test a draft of your response with the client before submitting.

You will use all of the skills and best practices in this book during this phase. They are SOCIAL STYLEs, Adaptive Selling, Decision Mapping, good Preparation, and possibly Baggage Handling.

Convince

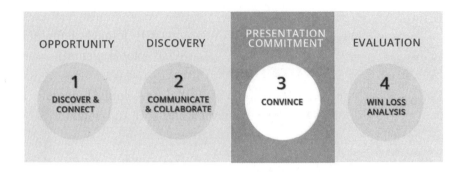

    The decision will be made during this phase. You are likely presenting your final proposal and presenting your solution orally. Ideally, you want to have two things as you enter into the Convince Phase. First, a solution that has been pre-tested with the client, and second, an accurate Decision Map. An accurate Decision Map will show you whom you must convince, what your messages should be, and the topics and order for your proposal and oral presentation. All of your skills and best practices should be used in this phase.

Win-Loss Analysis

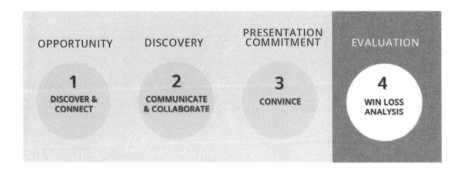

    Why did you win or why did you lose? You really won't know until you conduct Win-Loss interviews. All of your skills and best practices are again used in this phase.

SUMMARY

We have covered several topics and skills. The table below summarizes them, along with what we can learn from each.

SOCIAL STYLE	Self-awareness, needs of others, messaging, negotiating, and organizing by style. Result can be better relationships
VERSATILITY	How to improve and build better relationships and become a top performer
ADAPTIVE SELLING	How to connect, build better relationships, and improve chances of winning regardless of your sales methodology
BAGGAGE HANDLING AND EMPATHY	Building better relationships and handling prior negative experiences
DECISION MAPPING	Better understand how decisions are made and direct strategy. The Decision Map is a dashboard for the deal.
PREPARING FOR IMPORTANT MEETINGS/PRESENTATIONS	Especially on the "soft side," greatly improve the chances of winning and reduce stress and errors.
WIN-LOSS REVIEWS	Learn what you did well and what you need to improve

Final Thoughts and Comments

We have asked folks who read this book—and who had not been through any of our training—about what they learned. Here are some of their responses:

"I realized that I have been selling to myself all this time."

"We have been approaching first meetings the wrong way."

"I just lost a very competitive bid; I can see why now."

"The preparing for meeting section has been especially useful."

"We've never taken the time to analyze how decisions are made. Now I have a systematic way of doing this."

"I have been very guilty of talking and telling versus asking, listening, and probing."

"People who have attended training have seen the very same things. Those who have been profiled add that they now understand themselves and others better. Many have told me that they understand their spouses better!"

So, in addition to a sales-oriented book, the world now has a book to improve marriages, family relationships, and any situation where working effectively with others is required!

May you find Adaptive Selling a convenient addition to your sales tool kit and a powerful accelerator to your sales success.

ADDITIONAL RESOURCES

TRACOM Group – The Creator of SOCIAL STYLE®

The TRACOM Group—www.tracom.com—has several instruments and many useful publications; a few are listed below.

Contact information:

TRACOM Group Headquarters
6675 South Kenton Street, Suite 118
Centennial, CO 80111
U.S. Phone: (800) 221-2321 or (303) 470-4900

Recommended Publications

On their website, the TRACOM store lists many good books and reference guides. I would like to point out the following two in particular:

- *The Versatility Factor* by TRACOM's CEO John Myers and

Dr. Henning Pfaffhausen. This is the book on SOCIAL STYLE and Versatility if you only buy one.

• Another excellent book from TRACOM is *Enhancing Emotional Intelligence with Style Guide.*

Here are several other books on our bookshelf:

- *People Styles at Work* by Robert and Dorothy Bolton
- *Working with Emotional Intelligence* by Daniel Goleman
- *SPIN Selling* by Neil Rackham
- *Insight Selling* by Mike Schultz and John E. Doerr
- *Strategic Selling* by Robert B. Miller and Stephen E. Heiman
- *The New Conceptual Selling* by Robert B. Miller and Stephen E. Heiman

Versatility: Linkage to Emotional Intelligence

In 2003, TRACOM developed a new method for measuring SOCIAL STYLE and Versatility by creating the SOCIAL STYLE Profile–Enhanced (SSP-E). A major aspect of this revision was the emphasis placed on measuring more specific components of Versatility. Research in the area of emotional intelligence has led to a desire for updated research and expansion of the concept of Versatility. Recent publications (Bar-On, 2002; Cherniss & Goleman, 2002; Goleman, 1998; Goleman, McKee, & Boyatzis, 2002) have illustrated that TRACOM's concept of Versatility, originally developed in the 1960s, precedes and parallels many of the concepts of emotional intelligence. For example, one central aspect of the application of the SOCIAL STYLE Model is to "Know Yourself, Control Yourself, Know Others, and Do Something For Others." These correspond very closely to the four dimensions of emotional intelligence outlined by Goleman and his colleagues: Self-Awareness, Self-Management, Social Awareness, and Relationship Management. In addition, several of the competencies that compose the overall concept of emotional intelligence are very similar to those that define TRACOM's Versatility concept (e.g., Conscientiousness, Empathy, Optimism).

Training program participants can now receive an enhanced report that describes specific components of Versatility (i.e., Image, Presentation, Competence, and Feedback). This more detailed level of feedback is instrumental in helping participants to identify the specific behaviors that they should focus on in order to leverage their overall Versatility.

In 2004, TRACOM developed a follow-up measurement and feedback tool, the Versatility Report & Improvement Guide (VRIG), to provide people with a means for reviewing and practicing the Versatility information they learned during the workshop. Like the SSP-E, the VRIG measures components of Versatility in depth and provides even more detailed feedback and practical advice in the report. This has been replaced by The Versatility Check-up.

Similar to the principles of the emotional intelligence literature, one of the foundations of the SOCIAL STYLE Model that has been taught in TRACOM's courses over the past three decades has been that a person's particular Style counts less than the way he or she *uses* that Style when interacting with others. A person's level of Versatility indicates the degree to which he or she is perceived by others as focusing on reducing his or her own tension, or on reducing the tension of others. Will a person's actions be self-serving and focus more on personal comfort and tension reduction, without clear concern for the impact his or her behavior has on others? Or, will the person's actions demonstrate some degree of concern for reducing the tension in others, varying responses to maximize effectiveness for a productive relationship?

If a person creates a positive impact upon others with his or her Style, others will tend to report favorably about that person's actions. Like other researchers in the area of emotional intelligence, TRACOM has always asserted that Versatility is *changeable* and can be influenced through *training*. Versatility is the aspect of a person's Style that is most changeable and therefore most amenable to training and development, and the one that is most important for earning the endorsement of coworkers and others.

In order to develop the expanded Versatility model, a comprehensive review of the emotional intelligence literature was conducted, and several key concepts were identified as useful expansions of the Versatility measure. These concepts were clearly defined in relation to the Versatility components, and items were written to measure them.

When reviewing the emotional intelligence literature, certain criteria were established for selection of constructs that would correspond with and complement the Versatility dimensions. It was determined that each construct should:

- Have empirical support for its measurability.

- Have theoretical and empirical support for its relationship with interpersonal interactions and job performance.

- Theoretically fit into the existing conceptualization of Versatility.

Emphasis was put on adopting only those constructs that are most important for interpersonal skills and success within the workplace. The emotional intelligence framework is concerned with multiple facets of people's lives. While participants in TRACOM training programs often remark that the SOCIAL STYLE Model is relevant beyond the workplace, we wanted to maintain our emphasis on productive relations and functioning within the work environment. The table below shows the breakdown of sub-dimensions that are measured under each of the four Versatility components. These sub-dimensions include both the pre-existing Versatility constructs, as well as the newly adopted emotional intelligence constructs.

Image	Presentation	Competence	Feedback
Dress and Grooming Physical Workspace	Clarity of Communication	Conscientiousness Flexibility Innovation Perseverance Optimism Self Confidence	Active Listening Adaptive Communication Empathy Interpersonal Relations

Versatility Constructs Measured by the SSP-E and VRIG

References

Bar-On, Reuven. "Emotional and Social Intelligence: Insights from the Emotional Quotient Inventory (EQ-I)." In Reuven Bar-On and James D.A. Parker (Eds.), *Handbook of Emotional Intelligence*. San Francisco: Jossey-Bass, 2000.

Cherniss, Cary, and Daniel Goleman. *The Emotionally Intelligent Workplace: How to Select For, Measure, and Improve Emotional Intelligence in Individuals, Groups, and Organizations*. San Francisco: Jossey-Bass, 2002.

Goleman, Daniel. *Emotional Intelligence*. New York: Bantam
     Books, 1995.

Goleman, Daniel. *Working with Emotional Intelligence*. New York:
     Bantam Books, 1998.

Goleman, Daniel, Annie McKee, and Richard Boyatzis. *Primal
     Leadership*. Boston: Harvard   Business School Press, 2002.

CLIENT FEEDBACK ON ADAPTIVE SELLING

Does Adaptive Selling Work in the Real World of Clients?

Every sales leader evaluates sales methodologies and training with an underlying skepticism. "Does this really work?" "Will people apply it?" and "Will it lead to more business?" These are tough but good questions that deserve an answer. And the best answers come from people and organizations who have actually implemented a solution under consideration.

One of the best aspects of our work is the chance to interact with high-level professionals across a wide range of industries and learn of their experiences with Adaptive Selling and SOCIAL STYLEs. The following pages share their responses to a variety of questions regarding what outcomes they have seen in their organizations, their people, and themselves. These sales professionals have been using SOCIAL STYLEs to improve their own and their organization's ability to sell adaptively and to improve performance for between five and 30 years.

How do SOCIAL STYLE and selling adaptively add value to your sales methodologies?

"Many of the sales processes and methods in the market today are fine and they can work. What they typically do not address is EQ, the softer set of selling skills that are required to be consistently successful in sales. And that comes at you from different dimensions. It's not just the client interactions. It's the pursuit team that you build on the selling side. It's the delivery leadership team and how they mirror the client from a SOCIAL STYLE standpoint, demographically, and from an organization-accountability perspective"

— John Maguire
Senior Vice President, Chief Sales Officer - Cognizant

"Most sales type programs that focus on methodologies are all very similar. They're really about how do you understand your client or customer before you go meet with them. How do you make sure you ask really good questions? How do you provide insight? How do you develop mutually agreed next steps that then turn into opportunities? The key to success in sales for me, even more than a methodology, has been SOCIAL STYLEs."

— Jim Knauss II
Global Markets Leader - People Advisory Services - EY

"Of all the sales tools and methodologies that we've deployed, SOCIAL STYLE is the one that's landed the most effectively. It's interesting and easy to use. I see Style being used in our organization around the world. We see TRACOM as clearly being advantageous in a business development setting, but we see it as a much broader tool than that."

— Peter Matthews
Senior Partner

"There are a lot of sales training programs that I've taken. We have used different people all the time. So after going through all these programs, there is not anything about TRACOM's Style and Versatility that is in conflict with any of them. It enables every one of them. And it's a missing piece."

— Nancy H. Kopp
Director, Business Development - EY

"We thread SOCIAL STYLE through everything we teach. We have relationships with a variety of training companies whom we bring in for specific skills training. And over time, we've seen them adopt the concepts and use them, building on the concepts and tying their relevance to their content. For example, we use Franklin Covey for certain inquiry and dialogue skills in the sales process. Now when they teach in our programs they work with our participants to explain how their training can be applied when meeting with people of different Styles."

— Ernie Smith
Vice President Sales - Global Sales Process, Platform, Education, and Coaching - Cognizant

When did you first experience SOCIAL STYLE training?

> *"I started with SOCIAL STYLE almost 20 years ago. It is one of the foundational elements around which I build my sales education and training programs."*
>
> **— John Maguire**
> **Senior Vice President, Chief Sales Officer - Cognizant**

> *"Early in my career after I left teaching for business I was about to get fired. I hadn't sold anything since I started. It was May of 1989 and I was hired in November of 1988 and I hadn't sold a single thing. I got sent to SOCIAL STYLE training and I came out of that session and put that to work. The result was I sold so much that I was the top salesperson in EDS in my group by the end of the year. It made a remarkable difference for me."*
>
> **— Jim Knauss II**
> **Global Markets Leader - People Advisory Services - EY**

What impact has SOCIAL STYLE made on you personally?

"There's no question about the value of SOCIAL STYLE. I can tell you unequivocally and without a doubt that if it hadn't been for the Style training I took, I wouldn't be where I am today and have had the career success I have enjoyed. There's just no way. It has been that one critically important skill that I think has made all the difference for me."

— **Jim Knauss II**
Global Markets Leader - People Advisory Services - EY

"By applying SOCIAL STYLE in my work, I started to have individuals say to me: 'You've shown more concern for me than anyone else in my career, you helped build my confidence and helped me advance my career progression." So in a one-to-one situation, I made an impact and that was largely the result of SOCIAL STYLE. More importantly, in a team environment I became a bit less vocal, less concerned about grandstanding, less focused on only getting my point across. I became more comfortable to sit and listen and then contribute to the team discussion at appropriate points. Whereas before it was sort of 'ready, fire, aim,' what SOCIAL STYLE did was to help me recalibrate my approach. I became more 'ready, aim, fire.' As a result, I was more effective in influencing team discussions."

"I was better able to play a more active and constructive role as a team player as well as a coach. SOCIAL STYLE and Versatility impacted these two things in particular. And the feedback I received during my time at EY really confirms the significant impact I was able to make in both one-to-one coaching situations, and in a group or team environment. These are the areas where I think I have made a professional leap as a result of my SOCIAL STYLE training."

— **Andrew Wright**
Director - Vinuela Consulting, Ltd.

How have you integrated SOCIAL STYLE into training at your organization? Where?

"We use The Consultative Process as core to our collaborative approach with customers. We've also had some sales teams invest in Challenger Seller, and all of the teams are investing to some degree in Challenger Customer. But the one thing that underpins all of that is SOCIAL STYLE. Every sales person has it on their onboarding plan. Certainly we see references to it throughout our call prep, opportunity management, and account planning as our sellers consider who they're dealing with and what are the behaviors they're trying to influence with the individuals in their accounts. SOCIAL STYLE just weaves through all of what we do."

— **Fred Dulin**
Corporate Sales Director - Eastman Chemical Company

"Our sales training curriculum meets the needs of our organization and customers largely due to its customized content, which features SOCIAL STYLE and Versatility learning. Combining SOCIAL STYLE/Versatility with our Sales training has been a natural win-win."

— **Mike Miller**
Sr. Manager Learning & Development - Reynolds American, Inc.

"SOCIAL STYLE is part of the Cognizant way to sell. It's embedded into the way we sell. We use different outside firms and former CXOs in our sales instruction. We make sure everybody understands SOCIAL STYLEs and references back to it and how to use it. It is a fully integrated part of what we do, it's in our CRM system, and has become part of the dialogue at Cognizant."

— **John Maguire**
Senior Vice President, Chief Sales Officer - Cognizant

Do you have specific examples of how SOCIAL STYLE has benefited you?

"When I was starting out as a management consultant, I was meeting a new client in the city of London. I started off by saying; 'Hello Nigel. Nice to meet you. I am Peter Matthews...' He barely shook my hand, then said, 'Never mind that! How are you going to help grow my business?' I was in my mid to late-20s when that happened and Nigel was late 30s or early 40s. Understanding SOCIAL STYLEs stopped me from panicking. I was able to immediately see his behavior was not bad, not right, and not wrong. It was just how Nigel behaved. Therefore I focused very clearly on responding to the behaviours of a Driving Style. As a consequence I actually got the work and for many years I was Nigel's principal advisor."

— Peter Matthews: Senior Partner

"When I first arrived at a particular company I was brought in to drive a sales and marketing transformation program. I'm an Expressive Style. And very early on I was presenting the transformation plan to my CEO. He was asking really good, penetrating questions: very detailed and very deep into the process. After a number of these I said, 'Boss, I want to explain something to you about me. I'm an Expressive Style and you are an Analytical and while all the questions you are asking me are good and very appropriate, I'm going to get the bends coming up when this conversation is over. I can't have this level of conversation without my team. If you want to go this deep, I'm going to bring in some people who can answer those questions for you.' He just looked at me because I'm sure nobody had ever said anything like that to him. He looked at me and just started laughing and said, 'Okay.' I went on to say, 'What I do is, I paint the picture for a transformation and bring in the Driving and Analytical Styles to work with me to get the programs done. That's how I build teams internally as well as with clients."

— John Maguire
Senior Vice President, Chief Sales Officer - Cognizant

"SOCIAL STYLE has had amazing results on my career. About every three to five years, I report to someone new and they're always an extremely different style. And I've always been able to flex to them over time. Also, I'm in one of those roles where every week I could be working with new people. The nature of my work is in a national role so every year, even every trip, I am meeting brand-new people for the very first time. And the only way that I can drive the type of initiative that I do in my job is to build a large powerful network and have really strong relationships. And TRACOM helps me achieve that."

— Nancy H. Kopp
Director, Business Development - EY

How would you explain SOCIAL STYLE in 30 seconds to someone who's never heard of it?

"SOCIAL STYLE is unquestionably a very powerful way of looking at the world. It's clear, it's memorable, and it's something that you can apply quickly as opposed to many other models. You only need to remember four Styles and how to work with each of them. Even in the heat of the moment you can quickly apply SOCIAL STYLEs to build a productive relationship."

— Peter Matthews: Senior Partner

"The way that I would explain SOCIAL STYLE is that it is the foundation of how we collaborate with others, both internally and externally. It's a tool that helps us to understand the behavioral preferences of our working partners and gives us direction on how to engage to have the greatest productivity and the best chance of really aligning across multiple stakeholders."

— Fred Dulin
Corporate Sales Director - Eastman Chemical Company

"If you could gain the magical interpersonal skills that would instantly enhance your ability to connect with your customers and co-workers like never before, would you be interested? If I said the same skills would also drive enhanced relationships with your friends and family, what would you say? TRACOM's SOCIAL STYLE and Versatility provides the Social Intelligence a person needs to honestly and authentically improve rapport, demonstrate enhanced leadership, and connect with those they interact with on a regular basis."

— **Mike Miller**
Sr. Manager Learning & Development - Reynolds American, Inc.

"What is SOCIAL STYLE? I go back to what I said originally. It gives you a Framework based on behaviors that you can reasonably, quickly assess and categorize into four different Styles. And with the Versatility aspect of it included, it allows you to understand the way you can adapt your own personal approach to better fit with a client or a boss."

— **John Maguire**
Senior Vice President, Chief Sales Officer - Cognizant

"The SOCIAL STYLE Model allows you to understand how you behave when interacting with others, to identify how they like to work, and then using this information, you can adapt your own behaviors to flex to their preferences allowing both them and you to be more effective. It makes it possible for one to achieve their results, for their clients to realize their results, and the firm to increase its business and doing this while at the same time building strong business relationships with clients and colleagues."

— **Tracy Embo**
Associate Director - EY

"*The SOCIAL STYLE Model is aimed at helping people build more effective and more productive relationships based on observable patterns of behavior. These patterns represent the behaviors which are most comfortable for an individual and which are commonly observed by others. I think that is really important. All human beings are different, have different preferred ways of working, and to my mind the Versatility construct helps people really understand the behaviors which can be flexed, or adjusted, and will contribute most to building more effective relationships. What SOCIAL STYLE is not attempting to do is analyze or change your personality. It is what it is. Rather, it is the behaviors you tend to exhibit in your day-to-day interactions that are your choice, and that is the real power of the model. Ultimately you will be judged by others on the behaviors you exhibit, not by your intentions: no matter how good they might be! So I would say it's a very powerful model for enhancing your interpersonal effectiveness.*"

— Andrew Wright
Director - Vinuela Consulting, Ltd.

"*SOCIAL STYLEs is a quick way to identify a person's preference and how they make decisions as well as how they take in information. The four quadrants in SOCIAL STYLE are all unique styles and they all have their own preferences. By understanding the SOCIAL STYLE of someone, you are able to sell your ideas quickly based on the way they appreciate learning the information and getting to know you. This allows you to understand very quickly the strengths and weaknesses as you're talking to someone and the best way to sell your ideas.*"

— Anita Natesh
Sales Excellence Director, Americas - Eastman Chemical Co.

"I simplify the critical importance of SOCIAL STYLEs by an analogy. It is almost like I'm somewhere and I'm talking to people in English but they only understand a different language and there's no connection no matter what I could be telling them. If I say, here is a way to make a million dollars by just saying yes, they still won't act. Because they don't understand what I'm saying! They can't take advantage of the opportunity and SOCIAL STYLE is that way for you to very quickly flip into the ability to speak their language and be able to connect in a way people hear the message. So, no matter how great your message is, if it isn't delivered in a way that that Style will receive it and hear it then you're not going to be able to get anywhere with it. So I called SOCIAL STYLE 'The Great Interpreter.' "

— Jim Knauss II
Global Markets Leader - People Advisory Services - EY

What does the concept of Versatility mean to you?

"SOCIAL STYLE is about your effectiveness with your interpersonal skills, and what it does is it gives you an opportunity to find out how others perceive what you say and do versus what you think. And the most interesting thing about that is 53 percent or more people do not understand how they communicate. How their communications are perceived by others. Versatility is the most important part of it to me. Because I don't feel like in business you can accomplish much unless you meet the needs of others. So it just gives me a process for how to do that."

— Nancy H. Kopp
Director, Business Development - EY

"So to me the most powerful part of SOCIAL STYLE training is its Versatility aspect. Your Style is your Style: know it, be aware of it, good and bad. But really, Versatility is what really matters and it's a choice that everyone can make. People who have embraced it have come up to me long after going through the training and shared with me how adopting the principles has had a significant impact on improving their working relationships."

— **Ernie Smith**
Vice President Sales - Global Sales Process, Platform, Education, and Coaching - Cognizant

"Now personally, I feel an individual's ability to demonstrate strong Versatility, to flex their behaviors to meet the needs of others, is a critical attribute that propels good coaches and good salespeople to become superior leaders and award winning sales professionals. I feel Versatility has helped our organization drive our 'Others-centric' versus 'Me-centric' mindset. Versatility awareness and application has without question been a key contributor to our employee coaching success and award winning Sales function recognition. You've got to establish that rapport, create that collaborative partnership to earn the right to be your customer's trusted advisor. Only after this happens can both parties prosper."

— **Mike Miller**
Sr. Manager Learning & Development - Reynolds American, Inc.

"Versatility is a conscious choice to flex and adapt your Style to the needs of other people, making it easier for them to work with you. I also refer to it as your personal porch, how welcoming do you appear to other people. . . and make your porch as wide as possible to attract the biggest number of relationships."

— **Tracy Embo**
Associate Director - EY

"At its simplest, Versatility is a construct for helping people understand practical ways of increasing interpersonal effectiveness."

— **Andrew Wright**
Director - Vinuela Consulting, Ltd.

"SOCIAL STYLE takes on a totally different nuance from kind of the deep psychological underpinnings of why I'm the way I am. It's very, very different. MBTI and DiSC tend to be what I call psychological curiosities. You get a sense of this, I usually worked with MBTI and I think it's got great applicability to better understanding yourself. I think it's great but it's harder to remember and explain. And further, you're not really looking at how do I do something for other people so that, when extending a bit of myself to where they are behaviorally, they will then extend a bit of themselves toward me. It's that symbiotic relationship building that I think TRACOM really does a very nice job of. It is not just one and done, it is not who I am, here's one show up but it's now equipped with this information and what are you going to do about it. EY is so heavily invested in it and we see success going to those who exhibit Versatility. It's a real difference maker. Our sales business development team has embraced it, where it's the lingua franca of how they get things done."

— **David Bruesehoff**
Director, Talent Management - EY

"Versatility is key. You don't have to change your personality but modify the way you behave. Realize that the kind of signals you give to the
other person can really help or hurt your interaction. How versatile
you are determines the quality of interactions you have. It doesn't
mean you need to get along with everybody. It doesn't mean you won't
have challenges. And it's not a marriage saver or anything like that.
What it does for me, that knowledge of being able to walk into a room
and in minutes determine a person's Style, and then use that to align
how I'm going to treat them. That is key, and it works very well. So
that's what versatility is to me: being able to modify your behavior in
that moment with that customer or colleague or direct report or
management to be able to have a better quality of interaction."

> **— Tony Sammut**
> **Regional Sales Excellence Director - Eastman Chemical Co.**

"If you can't deliver your message in a way that another Style will
appreciate, listen, and understand it, then it doesn't matter what
you're saying. You could be telling them how to cure cancer but if
you're telling them in a way that somebody doesn't really understand
it because you're not doing it in their Style preference, you're not being
Versatile. It's not going to be received. And I think that's why SOCIAL
STYLEs in my opinion is the most important thing that somebody
needs to understand to be very good at selling, developing relationships, and managing accounts."

> **— Jim Knauss II**
> **Global Markets Leader - People Advisory Services - EY**

How would you say SOCIAL STYLE has affected your team(s)?

"In a professional services organization, you are thrown together with people on different projects that you've never worked with before. Being able to understand each other through a common language like SOCIAL STYLE drives better teaming and better trust. Another benefit is, the more trust there is within the team, the more that will come across to the client, and therefore the more likely we are to win the work."

— Peter Matthews: Senior Partner

"I think the big validation of the impact of SOCIAL STYLEs at the firm is how many people have come back to me and said they had a meeting set up and before we went in we really looked at this person's Style and formatted our discussion in a way that focused on their Style preferences. And it worked really well and helped us advance the business."

— Jim Knauss II
Global Markets Leader - People Advisory Services - EY

"Several years ago, I had a top sales person on my team who was meticulous at call planning and really embraced SOCIAL STYLEs as part of that prep. One of the things that she would talk about in planning the call was 'this person is this particular SOCIAL STYLE, and I know it because I see these types of behaviors and hear this type of language.' Then, as she got into the meat of the call prep, she would lead us through a discussion: 'So here's what we're trying to get across to them or ask them to do, considering that this person is a Driving Style, this is probably how we ought to try to orient the conversation.' So, she was very thoughtful in her planning and SOCIAL STYLE was at the core of much of her thinking. She was a strong Expressive Style, thinking about people a great deal, so using Style was just something that became very routine for her. It was part of her cadence in how she prepared herself. And she had great success in her career."

— Fred Dulin
Corporate Sales Director - Eastman Chemical Company

What's the most memorable feedback you've received from people who have been trained to use SOCIAL STYLE?

"People comment to us about how SOCIAL STYLE really opens their eyes in their personal relationships."

— John Maguire
Senior Vice President, Chief Sales Officer - Cognizant

"A few months after facilitating the SOCIAL STYLE and Versatility training session, I received a phone call from one of the participants in that class. He called me simply to tell me how impactful the class was to him both professionally and personally. And then he went on to tell me that immediately after the class he went home and began to implement and embed these skills in his daily conversations with his wife. The next thing he told me was 'Mike, I honestly believe that class may in fact save my marriage.' He thanked me and our organization for investing in our employees with development programs that benefit them professionally and personally. Obviously I was blown away, and his comments certainly made my day!"

— Mike Miller
Sr. Manager Learning & Development - Reynolds American, Inc.

"We have a big annual event in Florida. People come from all over the world and often grab me to talk about SOCIAL STYLE and what they can do to improve their Versatility. And the next time they see me it's to talk about what things they adopted, and how their relationships have gotten better. It really resonates with our professionals."

— Ernie Smith
Vice President Sales - Global Sales Process, Platform, Education, and Coaching - Cognizant

"The most memorable feedback I've received from people who have been trained to use SOCIAL STYLE is, 'you know what, I tried it and it works.' "

—Tracy Embo
Associate Director - EY

"Some of the best stories that I have heard have been outside of work. As my 20-year-old daughter has grown up, it definitely has come into play. It's a universal tool that applies with customers, colleagues, and one's family and friends."

—Fred Dulin
Corporate Sales Director - Eastman Chemical Company

"I'll never forget, shortly after I had a meeting with our business leader for the West, I was in L.A. for a different purpose, and he was in his office and on his white board he had the model of the four SOCIAL STYLEs, and they had some target they were looking at and how they were going to approach the target and who would be best to align with this first encounter. I turned to him and said, 'So, you guys really use this' because when you learned from the consultants you get a little suspicious; like is it really that way or is this consultant talk and to see him and his team actually embracing it as kind of a day to day, this is our common language, it's how we assess potential clients or expanding scope with clients. That says something. It's not like there's a program that stands behind the business development team and says you have to use this. This is just when you see that organic use of a tool you know it must have applicability, and of course, I've used it personally too at home, at work."

—David Bruesehoff
Director, Talent Management - EY

"I tell people after Style training to try a few experiments: find a customer who's a difficult person you have to deal with and you are not getting anywhere with them. Just try using Styles. And then they go and check out the person's Style: 'I think they are a more Analytical or Driving Style and what they need is...' Then they go out and try it and come back and say 'You know what? It works!' It works, and they come back just absolutely amazed. So most of my experiences have been very credible, very strong when people put it to work."

— **Tony Sammut**
Regional Sales Excellence Director - Eastman Chemical Co.

"I've had more than one person say it's absolutely the most effective and the most powerful program that they have ever been through. Because it's easy to understand and easy to learn and you can immediately start to apply it. Most professionals really want self-awareness and Style provides it with the skills to put it to work."

— **Nancy H. Kopp**
Director, Business Development - EY

"I had a senior partner who came up to me after the training session and said, 'I wish I'd taken this 20 years ago. It would have transformed my career.' There have been several people who have said to me that this has been the most powerful and most practical course they have ever attended in terms of helping them be more effective as a professional. When somebody comes up to you and is quite considered and pointed in their feedback, you take notice. I've had several people say 'I wish I had this training 10 years ago,' or 'Why am I getting this now.' It felt a little accusatory: 'Why did you wait till now to give me this tool?' You knew there was some frustration there. There is no doubt that the training has caused many people to recalibrate how they were interacting with others in a way they had not thought about before, and I think that is really important. Any training to have had that kind of impact is a testament to the power of the model."

— **Andrew Wright**
Director - Vinuela Consulting, Ltd.

What's specific business results can you share where SOCIAL STYLE was a contributing factor to gaining business?

"Back in my days at a previous employer, we had people that rescued troubled accounts. One of them came to our marquee training program where he learned and really embraced the whole concept around SOCIAL STYLE. He asked me go to his account to train his entire team because part of the problem at his current assignment was the poor internal dynamic of his Team was bleeding into the client relationship. After completing SOCIAL STYLEs training, they started understanding each other better and it created a much more productive environment. And he said that transferred into the account relationship within weeks. I think the prognosis when he got the account was it was going to be shut down but he actually saved the account. He would argue, I'm sure, that going through Social Style training was the beginning of what made them be able to deal with their differences, build better working relationships, because they were aware of those things that SOCIAL STYLE teaches. Financially, saving this troubled account allowed a continuing annual revenue stream of between 30 and 35 million dollars."

— Ernie Smith
Vice President Sales - Global Sales Process, Platform, Education, and Coaching - Cognizant

"I've seen wins in both my clients and others involving tens of millions of dollars of business that clearly have been influenced by applying SOCIAL STYLE and being Versatile. It's a common theme when we win. When a client trusts our team, we gain business. Given that SOCIAL STYLEs is our preferred way of training our people in how to build effective relationships, it's fair to say it's had a huge impact on our organization."

— Peter Matthews: Senior Partner

"We had a big change in the business that I was working in. We totally changed the way we do business. We had to get sales folks who were specification sales people and they now had to go downstream. They had to go approach different areas where we had never been before, with different people buying from us; they had never had to deal with us before. The feeling is that we would not have been as successful as we are today if we hadn't used this SOCIAL STYLE training. It wasn't about products because they weren't going to buy products. It was about selling value propositions and making personal connections with people across the value chain. So, if you didn't have Versatility, you would not succeed. If we hadn't had SOCIAL STYLEs and that training to work with, then the whole product approach would have failed, and it didn't. It was one of the most successful ever. SOCIAL STYLEs was one of many things we did, but I really believe that most people believe that if we hadn't had SOCIAL STYLEs we wouldn't have been successful with the launch and how we've done since then."

— Tony Sammut
Regional Sales Excellence Director - Eastman Chemical Co.

"To measure the performance of our Sales team function and training programs we regularly administer customer surveys which are conducted by independent 3rd party organizations. The surveys span coast to coast with many of our largest retail and wholesale customers. Customers are asked to compare our representatives and programs versus those of other top consumer goods organizations. When I look at the results of the surveys over the past eight years, we have been rated number one or two in every single category. It's something we're very proud of, and I know that our customized sales curriculum, which includes SOCIAL STYLE/Versatility, is a major factor."

— Mike Miller
Sr. Manager Learning & Development - Reynolds American, Inc.

"I witnessed SOCIAL STYLE having a great impact when a senior Partner, who was very Expressive, talked about the CFO of a major client who was very Analytical. Their relationship had deteriorated to the extent that the client would barely speak to the Partner. The Partner recognized that, having attended SOCIAL STYLE training, she needed to demonstrate much greater Versatility in the relationship, and specifically in the way she interacted with the CFO, if there was to be any chance of turning the relationship around and securing the business. The business on the table was significant so there was a lot at stake. The Partner really worked hard at focusing on improving her Versatility, responding to the CFO in a way that recognized his preferred way of working. While the Partner knew that her preferred way was to go 'full on' with lots of ideas, being very colorful and expressive in her language, the training helped her realize that continuing on that path would just have caused the CFO to retreat further. Over the next two or three months of working on her Versatility, the Partner was able to completely take the CFO into her confidence and re-build the trust. She did this by being more reflective, asking questions, listening, and giving the CFO more time to reach decisions. This eventually led to the Partner securing the business which, in her view, could have been lost to a competitor. This is a powerful example of working with SOCIAL STYLE and Versatility in practice. The training had a real impact on the senior Partner resulting in her re-thinking her approach to the CFO and in particular, what needed to shift in her own behavior in order to rebuild the relationship, to strengthen it, and most importantly, to re-build the trust."

—Andrew Wright
Director - Vinuela Consulting, Ltd.

"I would say SOCIAL STYLE has been part of an overall approach to winning business rather than the sole factor for success. I have used it on several multi-billion-dollar deals where I map the client buyers out, and figured out who on our team they were going to interact with. On one of those deals I had five strategic corporate partners on the team. I was the prime contractor, and because I had that much talent to choose from I could select the specific executives for the leadership team that matched up best with the client. Clients buy services deals when they look at the individuals across the table and say, 'I've got confidence that that group of people can get from where I am to where we want to be, to overcome my challenges and hurdles, and I actually would enjoy working with them.' So what I'm trying to do, what we teach our people is to mirror your delivery organizations as much as you can to the buyers and then make sure that there is a connection or relationship. That is how I've used it on very large deals and it makes a difference."

— John Maguire
Senior Vice President, Chief Sales Officer - Cognizant

"We have one customer that buys almost 50 million dollars from us. And we were able to maintain business and continue to grow it and continue to be a sole supplier. When we started out, they were telling us that they were going to be a dual-supplier customer and they did not want a sole supplier. But using SOCIAL STYLE helped us remain as their sole supplier."

— Anita Natesh
Sales Excellence Director, Americas - Eastman Chemical Co.

"A great example of success tied to SOCIAL STYLE was the salesperson I first referenced. We worked together on an innovation project, and landing that first alpha customer that would successfully use our product and bring it to the marketplace was critical. Until you have that, you really don't have credibility even within the company in terms of your innovation project. So, she was working with the alpha customer and it was a highly complex sale. There were a lot of people involved at the account, but there was one particular stakeholder that, as she did her work, she realized was going to be the key to determining whether they went commercial with the product that incorporated our new material. She identified his SOCIAL STYLE through spending time with him and talking to others in that gentleman's organization. She brought that back and not only used that understanding in her interactions, but she was also influencing vice presidents within Eastman about how they should be interacting with this client. She coached them on how they should be leaning, adapting their behaviors to be able to get the most of their work with that individual. And it worked! From the first meeting that we had with him up to the point of getting the commitment to actually move forward and beyond the launch, there was a huge shift in his willingness to engage with us. He wasn't in a position where he would typically engage with vendors. He wasn't a procurement person and he typically shied away from working directly with suppliers. But I think after he saw the value, not just the value that we brought, but the way that we were willing to engage with him, he really embraced us as a partner."

— **Fred Dulin**
Corporate Sales Director - Eastman Chemical Company

"I was speaking about an account with a senior partner and they shared how they used the SOCIAL STYLE approach in their account management. And I remember saying to him, 'You know you've got this relationship map and you've got yourself as the point for every single relationship.' He asked what I meant and I told him, 'You've got to have other members of the account team develop relationships with the different members of the executive client team. You need to really look at what are the SOCIAL STYLEs that can match up with the client.' I didn't know if he was going to act on that or not but about a year later I was at a conference and he came up to me and said, 'I want you to know, I was a little bit insulted at first but then I took it to heart and matched up people with different people in the account. We really focused on SOCIAL STYLE and how important that was. And we were able to win a whole lot more work and renew a contract. They told us we would have been fired from them if we hadn't done something differently on the account which we did. By simply aligning people who matched up SOCIAL STYLEs we gained significant business.' "

— Jim Knauss II
Global Markets Leader - People Advisory Services - EY

COMPARE YOUR INDUSTRY AND CHECK OUT YOUR MARKETS

TRACOM research looks at the interpersonal skills and Versatility of people in more than 30 industries. Each infographic shows the percentage of people who comprise each of the four SOCIAL STYLEs and the relative Versatility of that industry compared to others. While this research shows all Styles exist in every industry, you will notice that certain styles favor certain types of industries. Remember someone's Style is no indication of their success. It all depends on their Versatility!

The following pages summarize the findings of this research and provide:

• The distribution of each SOCIAL STYLE among workers (self-identified)

• The Versatility position of each industry among 24 industries ranked

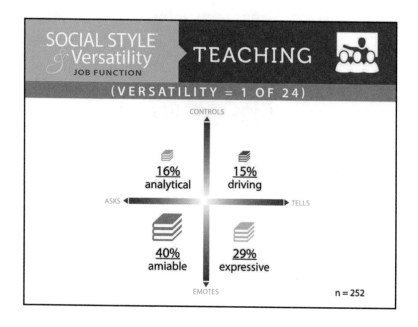

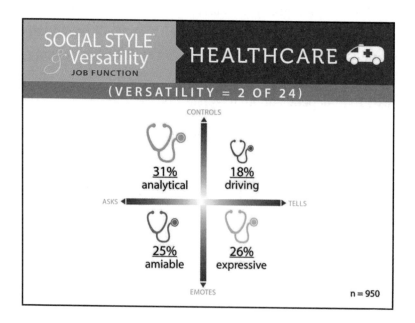

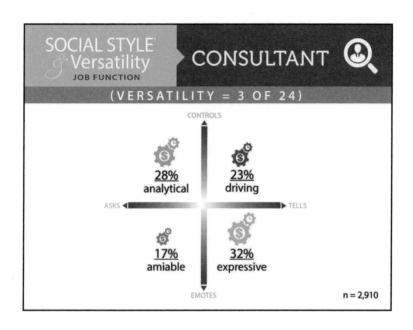

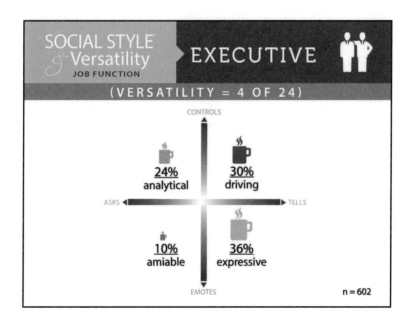

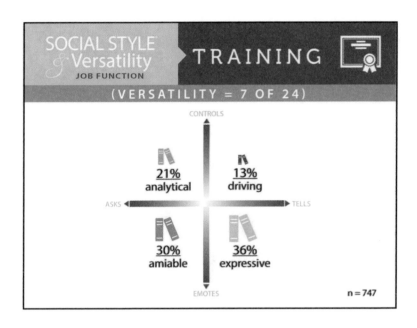

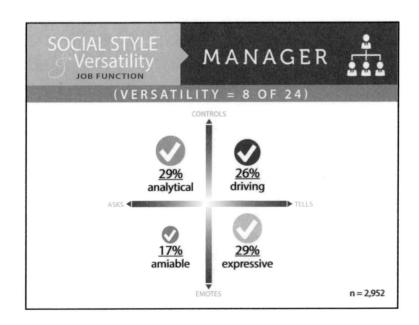

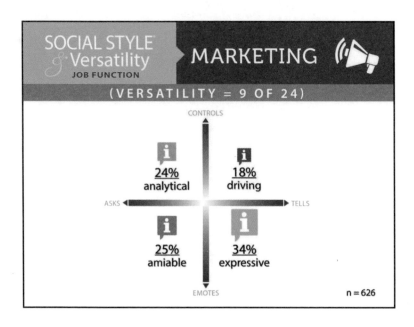

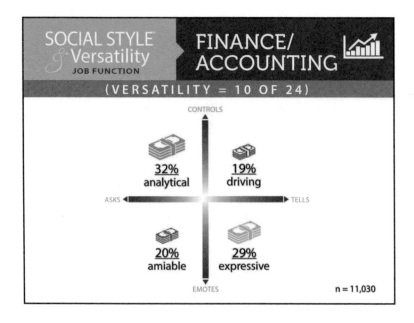

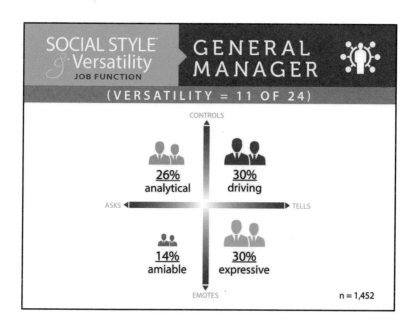

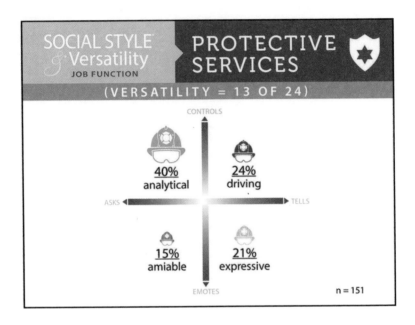

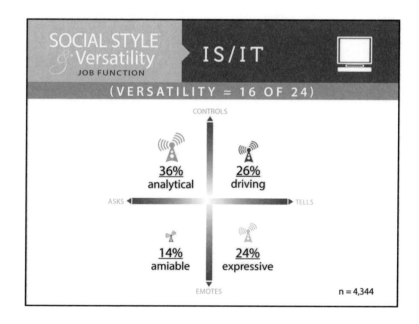

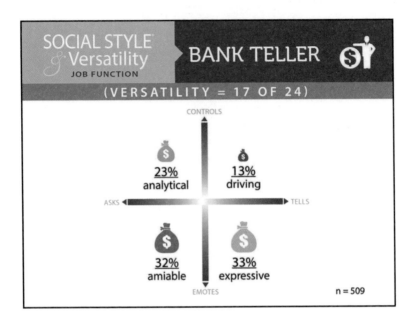

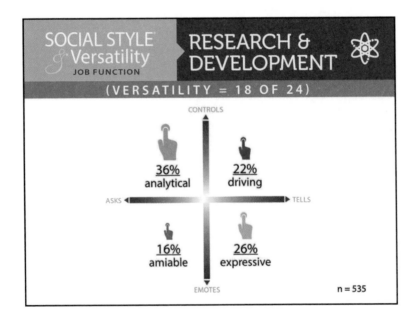

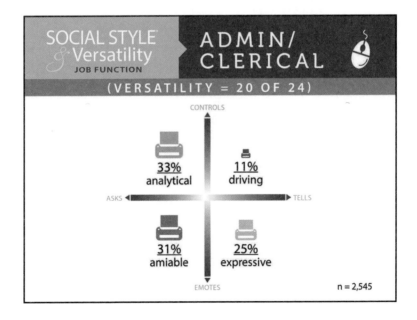

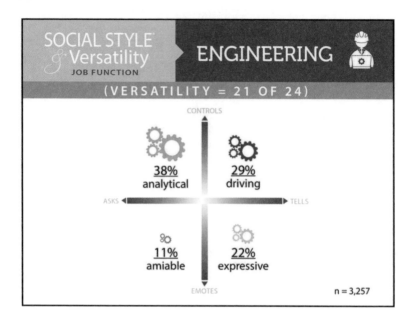

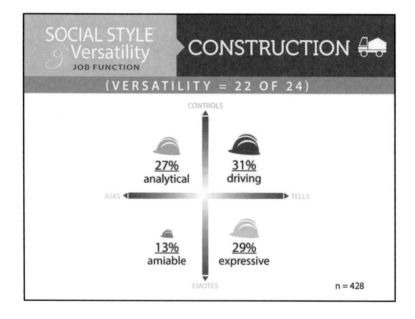

Endnotes

[1] LinkedIn Report on State of Sales 2018.

[2] Francis Gouillart and Bernard Quancard, The Co-Creation Edge (New York: Palgrave Macmillan, 2016).

[3] Https://www.brainyquote.com/quotes/zig_ziglar_617802. BrainyMedia Inc., 2019.

[4] 2017 CSO Insights World-class Sales Practices Report (Chicago: Miller Heiman, 2017).

[5] Daniel Goleman, Emotional Intelligence. (New York: Bantam Books, 1995).

[6] Effective Management through Interpersonal Skills Training (Denver: TRACOM Group, 2009).

[7] Emotional Intelligence Statistic. According to , a leading provider of emotional intelligence training, over 75% of the Fortune 500 companies use emotional intelligence training tools and 90% of top performers have high emotional intelligence.

[8] Adam Bryant, "How to be a C.E.O., From a Decade's Worth of Them," New York Times, October 27, 2017.

[9] Todd Kashdan, Curious?: Discover the Missing Ingredient to a Fulfilling Life (New York: William Morrow, 2009)

[10] Belinda Parmar, OBE, "Corporate Empathy is Not an Oxymoron," Harvard Business Review (January 8, 2015).

[11] Drew Boyd and Jacob Goldenberg, "Think Inside the Box," Wall Street Journal, June 14, 2013.